28|9

65

THE FACE OF VICTORY

LEONARD CHESHIRE, V.C.

THE FACE OF VICTORY

HUTCHINSON OF LONDON

HUTCHINSON & CO. (*Publishers*) LTD
178–202 Great Portland Street, London, W.1

London Melbourne Sydney
Auckland Bombay Toronto
Johannesburg New York

First published 1961

*This book has been set in Fournier type face. It has
been printed in Great Britain by The Anchor Press,
Ltd., in Tiptree, Essex, on Antique Wove paper
and bound by Taylor Garnett Evans & Co., Ltd., in
Watford, Herts*

To all those who
suffer and are in need
my wife and I jointly
dedicate this book

Author's Note

This is the story of an apprenticeship. Of course I realize that the whole of life is itself an apprenticeship, which will only find its consummation when we come to breathe our final breath. But the years which immediately preceed our embarking upon our life's work are in a very special sense an apprenticeship; and it is about these that this book is written.

When I began writing it I was alone: I had renounced all thoughts of a family life in order, as I believed, the better to devote myself to the needs of those for whom I was responsible. But later I married, and at that point my hopes and ideals found their fulfilment, for ours is a marriage not just of two people, but of two works: Sue Ryder's on behalf of the Forgotten Allies in Eastern and Western Europe, and mine on behalf of the chronic and homeless sick, now fused together into one and the same Mission for the Relief of Suffering, as we have chosen to call it. Not only have we discovered unexpected happiness and strength in our union, but we have each found it easier, I think, to broaden our interests and so to look at things from other people's point of view. Now, to claim a major share in our love and affection, we have our little Jeromy, barely six months old, and, because of him, the work to which we wish to devote our lives, far from suffering detriment or loss, has rather gained, for so mysterious are the ways of Providence that no true and legitimate love seems ever to detract from another, as if love, like water, becomes purer the more freely it flows, and indeed must flow ever faster and more freely in order to remain love at all.

To all those who appear in these pages—not always wholly identified—I offer my sincere apologies if I have, in any way, unwittingly misquoted them or misrepresented the part they have played in my life. To those who do not appear, yet who have also helped me so much, often to their own detriment—and there are very, very many—I humbly offer my sincere and heartfelt thanks. Only God can know how great a debt of gratitude I owe, not only for all I have received, but also for the mistakes from which I have been saved.

LEONARD CHESHIRE

Cavendish, Suffolk

I

THE war hit me at a most opportune moment. I was twenty-one, fired with all the enthusiasm of youth, horrified at the imminent threat of settling down to a lifetime of work, bursting with I don't know how many half-formed, untamed yearnings for a great and glorious career in which adventure and wealth were to be the principal ingredients.

In such a frame of mind the news that we were at war came as no disaster; rather the reverse—as a heaven-sent release, as a magic carpet on which to soar above the common-place round of everyday life. Yes, how I longed to soar, though where and how I do not quite know: how impatient I was for action to start; how eagerly I ran towards the post-man, looking for the call-up papers that were so slow in coming. At times, no doubt, I asked myself how I would stand up to it all; what would happen when I suddenly found myself in action, with the prospect of dying an imminent reality? But hardly had the question been asked than it answered itself.

For what thought does youth give to death? What part can death have with a body that feels itself fitter and stronger every day, that can defy so effortlessly the warnings of its elders: 'You can't burn the candle at both ends; you'll pay for it in the end, mark my words.' How can death, that shadowy phantom that even grandmothers gloss over as if it didn't

9

really exist at all, how can it expect to contend with the fire and vigour of youth, with those mysterious pulse-beats that vibrate so powerfully, springing from such hidden depths and reaching for such dizzy heights?

Let death look to others, let it even look to the whole wide world, but not to me. No, not to me. How many others have not set out from home with exactly these desires and exactly these thoughts? And how many will not continue to do so until the end of the world?

On the day war was declared I drove in to Oxford and bought a dozen rabbit snares so that Mother and Father could keep themselves fed when food was no longer to be bought. Then I dug a shelter for them. Actually I dug two, one out in the middle of the field, where it would be safer but more difficult to reach, and the other in the little pine wood twenty yards from the front door. Both were finished shortly after breakfast the following morning: but I needn't have been in such a hurry, for Air Ministry was sitting tight on my papers, even though I had been granted a Permanent Commission six weeks before, and there were no visible signs of enemy action.

When in early October I finally reached Flying Training School, I found myself plunged in a whirlpool of facts, figures, exams, flying schedules, and all that goes with a training institution. To begin with it had a sobering, almost chilling, effect.

Then came the news of the Russian attack on Finland. So powerful an aggressor against so helpless a victim. I put in an application to go and fight for the Finns. The Station Commander, whose name in those days was spoken amongst us with great respect, gave a sympathetic hearing but said 'No' very firmly. With the best will in the world a semi-trained pilot would be of little use, even to the Finns. Would a soldier be of any use who still needed to practise the mechanics of walking? No, the impulse was right, but the timing was wrong. First let me reach the point where flying came as easily as walking, then if there was something special to volunteer for he would see that I got it. The psychology was good. I walked out of the office with my chest a little higher and my mind made up. Henceforth everything could go by the board except training—*almost* everything that is, for it wouldn't do to be too serious. A good pilot must know how to play as well as work.

A good pilot! How much I wanted to be a good pilot, particularly when on June 6th, 1940, I reported in at the guardroom of R.A.F. Driffield, in Yorkshire, to join my first operational squadron. But I never was. Before the summer was out, when we had already completed our first twenty operational trips, some of the others said that if I were to fall into a cesspit I would come up with a gold watch and chain round my neck, and it was true; it made up for what was lacking in skill and experience.

War, like love, knows no law, answers to no logic. The suitor who offers the most convincing proofs of love or uses the most gallant turn of phrase does not necessarily carry the day. Nor does the best or most gallant pilot always carry off the greatest victory. A shell aimed at one aircraft hits another whose evasive action was far more professional and well thought out. Two crews go in to the same target, both equally well matched, both equally experienced in the art of aerial warfare. One comes back, the other does not. Those who seem strong, who give the impression of being beyond the reach of flak and fighter, unaccountably fail to return when others who look so ill-equipped, who never seem to inspire confidence, go stumbling from one victory to another. And even that is not the end of the matter, for amongst those whom fortune favours there are degrees of favour.

Two men may attend the same briefing and listen to the same intelligence report. One may conjure up a vivid picture of the defences, of what it will mean when they open up, and of how heavily the odds will be stacked against him; the other may give no thought to this, he may only be thinking what a beautiful sight it will be when the target goes up in smoke, as go it surely will. The former will require a hundred times more courage than the latter, but it will be the latter, almost certainly, who will bring off the more spectacular result. But even then only if luck is on his side.

Without luck the best, even the bravest, will not win the day or find his name amongst the list of honours. Such is the plain truth—for those who win a prize, a reminder that the credit is not wholly theirs; for those who win nothing, a consolation. But what is it, one may well ask, that lies behind the distinction? Is it that Fortune has no preferences, no power to judge between one man and the next, and merely lunges out, haphazardly and senselessly, like a roulette wheel? Or is it that she has her own mysterious designs, too deep for human mind to fathom? Is it that the story of human life is still incomplete, that there remains a final chapter in which all that is meaningless will make sense, all that is broken will be rejoined?

Yes, indeed, one may well ask. But who is qualified to answer? And what has a pilot to do with such questionings when there are the laws of flight, so relentless and uncompromising, to be mastered, the freedom of the skies to be gained, a global war to be fought and won.

As the war spread farther and farther across the world, it passed through many phases, some light-hearted, some tedious, some even a little tense. So long as it kept going, all was well; there was an enemy to fight, a standard to maintain, both of which demanded full-time attention. But unfortunately the war did not always keep going; there were periods when it hung fire, when there were no targets to attack and no operations to fly.

One of these came early on, in May 1941, when the Squadron was grounded for a hold-up in the delivery of its new four-engined Halifaxes and the crews were dispersed in various directions. My own posting was across the Atlantic to Montreal, where I was to wait for a Hudson to ferry back to England. The wait turned out to be a long one, and in order to kill time I hitch-hiked my way down to New York, minus authority or passport but nevertheless without much difficulty. New York had been my boyhood Utopia, the city of swing music and film stars and fabulous wealth, which one could dream and read about but never expect to visit in the flesh. How could I be so close and not make use of the opportunity? On leaving home I had stopped at the gate leading into the field and shouted out at Mother: 'I'll come back with an American wife.' It had been said to annoy her, for I knew only too well her views on this dreamland country of mine, but it was destined to come truer than I ever imagined.

When in the middle of July I landed back at Prestwick, in a Hudson with a leaking petrol-tank which barely gave us enough margin to taxi off the runway, I left behind a film-star wife, Constance Binney. Between us there was a difference of eighteen years, not to mention a completely different world, but somehow in the dazzling lights of New York, a hundred times the brighter by contrast with the black-out of London, that had not seemed to matter. And if there was the faint whispering of doubt at the back of either of our minds it was quickly stifled. Was, after all, marriage so irrevocable and final? Had not hundreds of thousands been contracted and dissolved and recontracted? Had not Constance been through the experience herself without coming to any harm? Was it not the healthy way to take the plunge, and if by bad luck it should turn out to be wrong, to acknowledge one's mistake and start again? Could there be any hard feelings, even any regrets, under such circumstances as these? No, of course not. So plunge we did, with two strangers—one from the lawyer's office and the other talked into it in the lift—as our witnesses and sponsors.

But others did not seem to think quite the same as we did. Curiously enough no one did. On arriving back at the Squadron the Adjutant met me with the words: 'Now it will be rather a different story, won't it? No more belly-aching to get into ops. No more applications for extension of tour. No more line-shooting about ops being the only life worth living.' And just to press his point home he jabbed me in the ribs with the full weight of his sixteen stone.

The point had not actually struck me, but now that he had come to mention it I sat up and took notice. He was a bluff sort of man, but just, and I liked him. And it was certainly true that I had done a great deal of wishful thinking about life after the war. The sooner I stopped that, the better. As it so happened, the Squadron Commander had his knife in me too, and when a daylight trip came up against Brest I was left off the crew list on the grounds of being too inexperienced. Rivaz, my rear gunner, was pinched for the C.O.'s crew, and I was sent off to Berlin in the company of four other aircraft from another Group 'to gain experience'.

It was long before the Berlin season, but they thought that if we went in on the Northern route via Denmark there would be enough darkness to get in and out without being caught by fighters. Just to add a little variety, we were given a new 4,000 lb. bomb which did not fit the bomb-bay and forced us to fly with the bomb-doors open. According to our calculations there was not enough petrol to make the long journey round and back, but this observation was not received with great enthusiasm. We were told to leave such matters to our elders and betters—who, one might add, were sending five inexperienced crews to face the combined weight of Berlin's defences, the heaviest in the world.

What with everything, we took off in not the best of tempers. The flak followed us intermittently from the coast onwards, but it was not unduly bad and there seemed no need for more in the way of evasive action than normal changes of course—to the discomfiture, it may be said, of the rear gunner, who said that this wasn't what *his* skipper did at all. On the way back, however, when an unusually large battery opened up, I felt a sudden urge to do something different and stood the aircraft on its nose, eliciting the most horrible language from the rear gunner, who had banged his nose on the gun-sight. But when the shells burst above us, exactly where

14

we would have been had we not dived, his flow of language changed abruptly into song: 'O, for the wings, for the wings of a dove.'

The rest of the crew burst into song too. We were back in harness once again. The star that had watched over us during the past year was still in the sky above us, bright, if not brighter, than ever before. Under such a light as that, what cause had we for worry; what opposition need we fear? And indeed, when a few miles inside the English coast the outboard engines cut through lack of petrol, there was not so much as a murmur from anyone, just a not very respectful aside from Jock Hill, the wireless operator, as we lined up for a priority landing with the inboard engines still mercifully running, and received a red from the Duty Control Officer.

Not long afterwards my brother Christopher went missing. He was two years younger than I, and ever since the day that I had escorted him to school as a new boy I had felt a strong sense of responsibility for him. I had watched his progress through the various stages of flying training with some trepidation, and had been horrified when he had been posted on to Halifaxes, which I considered quite unsuitable for anyone so young and innocent. The fact that he had made the grade and was reported as being perfectly capable of looking after himself had occasioned me considerable surprise, which was in no way lessened when, on the night that fog closed in over the whole country causing the loss of forty Bomber Command aircraft, Christopher was one of the few who managed to get his Halifax safely down.

Then, on his twenty-third trip, he failed to return. Under the best conditions it would have been bad enough, but these were not the best. Bomber Command was to blame; they had bungled the route, and sent us in to Berlin in a straight line between Wilhelmshaven and Bremen, which meant that all aircraft would be under fire from one side or the other, and those straying off track in great difficulty, especially on the way back and if already damaged. I tried hard to contact Christopher on the telephone and warn him to pay no attention to the official route, but I couldn't get through. No doubt it would have made no difference even if I had. But it might have, and I was angry. That night I landed in a great deal of trouble over Magdeburg, and at 1,800 feet, virtually out of control, gave the order: 'Stand by to bale out.' But when Jock, the wireless op., shouted back: 'Come on, Mr. Cheshire, you can do better than that!' I pulled myself together and scraped through. Poor Mother, had she received two telegrams on successive days.

By the time Constance arrived in England life had regained its old momentum; even the Adj had no complaint to make. What was more, we were well on the way to obtaining permission for low-level bombing of precision targets—a long-desired and advocated tactic. But unfortunately the Squadron received another set-back; there was trouble with the Halifaxes and operations were a rare occurrence. I myself was declared 'Tour expired' and grounded, but kept on the Squadron. I was neither fish nor fowl.

For a time there was the excitement of getting Constance installed in the expensive flat we had taken in Harrogate. There was also a Rolls-Bentley to drive about in, and a poodle puppy called Simon to steer away from my wardrobe. Christopher was reported safe and sound. What with one thing and another the time passed reasonably smoothly until Christmas. But with the New Year the rot set in. First I grew restless, then touchy and unsociable.

In early spring I was posted to the Operational Training Unit at Marston Moor and made a flying instructor. But not a very good one. In the first place instructors are expected to be methodical and textbook-minded; they are not encouraged, for instance, to do their cockpit drill while taxi-ing round the perimeter track, nor to run the engines up on take-off without halting at the end of the runway. In the second place training units are by no means operationally minded. Parades are a matter of almost weekly occurrence; senior officers, especially if they happen to be administrative, are treated as if they were actually important people; to kiss one of the W.A.A.F.s under the mistletoe on Christmas morning in a half-dead and empty Mess is sufficient breach of discipline (as I learnt to my cost) to warrant a week's orderly officer duty. Constance, however, who had finally devised a means of compressing her outsize in wardrobes into the confines of a Harrogate flat—and her American sense of humour and fun into that of a wartime spa —was now confronted with a three-storey barnlike country house, which even two pantechnicon loads of furniture could not succeed in filling, and the solitude of a partially evacuated country village. All in all, life was difficult and tedious.

Then one day, when I was lying propped up in bed in some temporary quarters on a remote satellite aerodrome, recovering from 'flu, the C.O. walked in (to my considerable surprise) and said:

'We've got a new Squadron to form, and I reckon you're the only man who can do it.'

'Nuts.'

'I beg your pardon.' He looked genuinely taken aback.

'Actually, I said nuts. It's a polite way of saying that I beg to differ.'

'Well, mine's a polite way of telling you that you're no longer needed. You've been promoted to Wing Commander, and posted!'

Which shows how anxious someone must have been on the move. But no matter, the incarceration was over; and how full and varied the freedom that was to follow!

There was the attack on Karlsruhe, our first operation as a fully formed Squadron, when we were detailed as the first of the Master Bombers and found ourselves watching one of the most successful attacks of the war. There was the vast, dazzling explosion of the ammunition dump at Wilhelmshaven, which had literally turned night into day for the matter of ten or fifteen seconds. But there was also the cloudless, moonlight night on the way back from Genoa, when with the automatic pilot in charge, my feet up on the instrument panel, and half the crew asleep, an Italian fighter had closed to thirty yards, without the rear gunner so much as firing a shot or opening his mouth, and missed. It was the rear gunner's first trip, so we asked him very politely if he would mind being a little more vocal next time the fighter came in to attack. But no. Not a shot, not a shout; just a sudden stream of tracer between the cockpit and the nacelle, which looked as if it couldn't possibly miss, but somehow did—but then only through slamming back the two starboard motors and standing on the starboard rudder, a manœuvre which we had practised hour after hour in the peaceful Yorkshire skies, to the great dislike of Jock, the wireless operator, who maintained that it played havoc with his set.

Through thick and thin, through bad weather and good, we clung to this habit of practising. We practised flying, we practised our bombing, we practised our gunnery, we practised our evasive action, we practised our cockpit drill. We carried out experiments to increase the safety factor of the aircraft, we thought up new tactics, we liaised with Fighter Command to try and steal a march on the German defences. And if we were neither operating, nor training, nor on duty in the Ops Room, we did what all sane pilots do—we beat it up.

On returning from one such party at the Half Moon, Willy Tait, the distinguished but shy holder of four D.S.O.s, somersaulted the car and shot me out on my head. I was taken to the Sheffield Head Injuries Hospital, where the doctor handed me a box of matches and asked me if I could read it. So, three days later, I escaped in disgust, and returned to the Squadron. But all cannot have been entirely well, for I found it difficult to keep awake and on four successive trips fell asleep immediately after leaving the target. Had it not been for the indignity of admitting that a doctor can after all be right, I might have reported sick.

But apart from all that, news had filtered through of Christopher. He had run into trouble over Berlin, had turned back early and been heavily engaged by the defences outside Bremen. After he had been badly hit and lost an engine, a shell had shot off his tailplane and sent the aircraft into a vertical dive; there was nothing for it but to jump. On arriving at the escape hatch himself—a difficult enough operation under such circumstances—he found the Flight Engineer behind him, and had stepped over the top to let him out first. If my young brother could do as well as this, then who was I to let a little sleepiness stop me flying?

When Christmas came round, the fourth of the war, everything was set to celebrate in true Air Force style; and celebrate we did. On returning from a pre-dawn tour of those on duty, doling out bottles of beer to all and sundry, I remembered three N.C.O. aircrew languishing in the guard-room under lock and key. I stopped the car, adjusted my cap at a sober and proper angle, and produced what remained of a crate of beer. Very soon we were drinking, police, prisoners, and all.

'You know,' I said to the Duty Sergeant of Police when the beer had begun to have its effect, 'I've never been able to understand how one gets a pair of handcuffs on a prisoner who feels like resisting.'

'Nothing to it, sir. You get him round the elbow, like this. Mind you, it wants to be with some strength. Bring the hand-cuffs down—like this. Kind of quick like. Then snap.'

But something evidently wasn't quite right, for there was a sort of bewildered look on his face. The ruse had worked. He was the prisoner of his own handcuffs.

'What a pity,' said Simon, bounding off with someone's forage cap, 'that the senior officers are all in bed, and can't join in on the fun.'

On April 1st, 1943, they took me off operations and gave me a new cap—with gold braid on it. The Station I was given to command was Marston Moor, where the administrative staff still cherished doubtful memories of a flying instructor whom, only six months before, they had recommended for a posting back to the squadrons; and it was with mixed feelings —almost with a feeling of loneliness—that I reported in at the guardroom. The quarters they allocated me were spacious and comfortable enough, but the floor under the lino was swimming in water, so I ordered a tent from the S.W.O. and moved out into it until the water was fixed. Hardly had I fallen asleep than I was woken by a loud voice which said:

'Who's in there?'

'The Group Captain.'

'Is he? Well, give me a brick.'

Then I discovered that I was expected to hold a weekly camp inspection, a twice-weekly C.O.'s parade and a daily orderly room, and that unless I learnt the King's Regulations by heart I would remain for ever under the thumb of the S.W.O. For the first time in my life I felt a twinge of sympathy for those who occupy the post of Station Commander.

The situation was slightly relieved by the arrival of Constance and the distraction of looking for a house. Houses were to be had easily enough, at a distance (and at a price), but not sufficiently close to keep a constant eye on the Station, as by nature and training all good Group Captains like to do. So we bought a railway carriage and installed it in a farmer's field barely a hundred yards from the Mess, where it was to give Constance's sense of art and improvisation the biggest challenge she had yet faced.

For myself—for the first time, I think, in my life—I felt completely a fish out of water. The work to be done, true enough, was no less important than that of the front-line squadron; but it *felt* less important. There was no visible enemy to fight, no emergencies to deal with; and once one has become accustomed to states of emergency, life without them becomes flat and dull. One looks within oneself for some source of inspiration to replace the missing stimulus from without. And if it should be missing, what does one do?

Partly in order to make the best of a bad job, but partly also to find some outlet through which to let off steam, I embraced the cause of aircraft serviceability (about which I knew nothing, other than the fact that it governed the number of flying hours the Station could do), and threw myself into it heart and soul. On the side of the hangar there appeared a large red pointer, such as one sees on the wall of dilapidated churches, which gradually rose towards a zero mark representing a given number of hours flown per mouth. The idea was that as soon as the pointer reached the target, which was a 20 per cent increase on the previous average, the Station closed down and everyone went on leave until the end of the month. For the first two months the scheme was a huge success, but it ran into difficulties when we came to fill in the leave returns, for higher authority pronounced that the procedure was illegal. So we were forced to look for an outlet in other directions. This we found in an unexpected way.

Reports had been coming in that the Germans were planning to neutralize Bomber Command's offensive by landing paratroops on its aerodromes. We were asked to take suitable precautions. And this we did to the utmost of our ability. The armoury was invaded for arms and ammunition; strongpoints were built and interconnected by telephone; permanent look-outs were posted; full-scale exercises, sometimes lasting all night, were held; and a variety of other measures were put in hand. When a Commando training unit asked permission to 'raid' the Station, adding that it had been done often enough before and that none of us would be any the wiser for it having taken place, we looked extremely bored and told them they could do as they liked. But we mobilized every available man and woman to hold them at bay, and gave them a good run for their money. When three Bren-gun carriers from Northern Command strayed by mistake into the aerodrome, they were very surprised indeed to find themselves rounded up by five armoured cars, antiquated enough in appearance, but manned by armed airmen who left no doubt at all about their intentions.

Meanwhile out in the world the war was being waged with ever greater intensity. In the Far East the Navy had succumbed to the Japanese Air Force; Singapore had fallen; even India was in jeopardy. In the Near East a major battle was raging; the German Army was on the point of being thrown back into the Mediterranean. In Russia there was a reversal of fortune; the Luftwaffe was losing its superiority; the Blitzkreig had reached the limit of its trajectory and was boomeranging back against those who had launched it. In the West there was talk of a vast American build-up and of a Second Front in the offing. Everywhere there were signs that the climax was rapidly approaching. From Bomber Command itself came news of a revolutionary form of raid by a specially formed and equipped squadron of volunteers. On their first attack they had destroyed the heavily defended and allegedly impregnable Mohne Dam. What would they do next? So much was happening, so much remained to be done, and we so far out of it all, so utterly useless, frittering our time away on goodness only knows what.

Even so, Marston Moor was not without its pathos and its drama; for death was a frequent visitor to the airfield. It had been, of course, a far more frequent visitor on the squadrons; it had walked a thousand strong and more down in the misty and fiery depths below us; it had haunted the skies above us until those who remained from the early days of 1940 could be all but counted on the fingers of two hands. But that had been a different death altogether, far more impersonal, far more remote. Here was a death that one could touch, and see, and smell. No more painful than the other death, no doubt, but so close, so visible, and invariably accompanied by fire.

One day, when an aircraft caught fire in the air and tried to regain the airfield—in spite of our desperate instructions not to do so—I found myself on the scene of the crash a matter of seconds after it had taken place. Picking his way through the wreckage and the fires I saw a man, though who it was I could not tell. I stopped beside him to see if he needed help, decided that he didn't, and ran on to look for others who did. But I found none; they were all dead. As soon as the rescue squad had finished its work and gone, I walked up to the doctor who was standing bareheaded by an ambulance:

'Who was the survivor, Bob?'

'The survivor? There isn't one. Just seven bodies.'

'But I know there is one because I saw him; he was picking his way through the wreckage over there.'

'We found him by the hedge. But he was killed instantly; his back is broken.'

I had heard of people charging their enemy and carrying on to their objective in spite of being mortally wounded; in fact Jack Randle, with whose help I had climbed back into college in the early hours of the morning so often, had done exactly that and been awarded a posthumous V.C. for doing it. But I had never heard or dreamt of this, a man already dead yet deliberately threading his way through a series of obstacles. What did it mean?

Was it that death, not content with victory itself, demanded its amusement and satisfaction as well? Or was it that death's victory was not final; that there existed some unseen power— either within man or outside him—with which to conquer this last enemy too? According to the clergy, the latter. But if so, then why speak in hushed and awed terms, as if to make certain that no one else was listening? Why preface what is said from the pulpit by an expression of apology or quasi-doubt, as if it were just a personal opinion: 'Surely it is to be believed?' Why not speak out in the manner and voice of a conqueror, certain of themselves and their cause, heralding the victory in which they believe, and in whose cause they have sacrificed so much?

2

WHEN the news came through that I could revert to operational flying and had been given command of 617 Squadron—the Dambusters, as it was popularly called—Constance went completely off the deep end, and for two weeks we remained at loggerheads. It was not so much that there was yet another (and unnecessary) period of danger and separation to come; nor that the move involved a drop in rank which Air Ministry had awarded only as a special concession and in deference to the A.O.C.'s request; nor that the railway carriage had only just been made reasonably habitable and comfortable and would now have to be abandoned; but that I had said it was too comfortable. And so, taking the circumstances into consideration, it was. For if one wants to fight—and God knows that I did—one despises comfort; one has to. One forgets how but only a short while back comfort was so all-important, so exacting in her claims. Curious how fickle are one's attachments, and how quickly they change to suit one's changing moods and objectives. Father, who had never expressed himself with violence before, now took sides with Constance, and with greater effect because of his astonishing command of English and his gift for logical exposition. Did I, he asked, seriously think that the few extra bombs I could drop myself, no matter how skilfully or courageously, would make any difference to the winning of the war? Could I not see that experience so hardly won was not one's own to scatter recklessly to the four winds, but belonged to the country to dispose and command as she thought best? Hadn't I the wit to understand that to keep experience to oneself was to frustrate its purpose, it was to stultify its growth, to condemn it to perpetual stagnation? And come to that, wasn't I over-estimating my own capabilities? Wasn't twenty-five a bit old for a special duties low-flying pilot; shouldn't that be left to the fittest and the strongest, who were at the beginning and not the end of their career? Had I, in fact, not taken clean leave of my senses? Could I not see that what I was proposing was nothing short of madness, sheer madness?

Yes, no doubt it was. No doubt cold, sober reason demanded that one stay put—a pundit among pundits. But in a world so full of planning, so anxious to administer, so adept at calculations, is there not room for a little madness; or place for the heart, not the intellect, to take charge? And does a bird just freed from captivity stop to listen to warnings? Does it worry at the thought of prowling cats or hovering hawks, or at the possible disappointment of those who used to gape and stare at it? Mother understood this only too well. She said:

'Leave the boy alone. It's his own life. Let him make up his own mind.'

And make up my mind I did.

617 was strictly for volunteers only, and for those who had completed their full quota of two operational tours at that. Its members had almost all dropped a rank in order to qualify, and therefore the Squadron had a discipline and an attitude of mind towards senior officers all of its own. It also had a casualty rate all of its own—seven out of sixteen on the dams, six out of nine on the Dortmund-Ems. Of the original eighteen crews there remained only four to carry on the spirit and the low-flying technique. When I went round the Command looking for volunteers for my crew, I met with a surprising lack of enthusiasm—but perhaps largely because they were uncertain as to how the Captain would stand the test. Even

the old stalwart Jock, who for the best part of two solid years had baulked at nothing, dug his toes in firmly and said:

'No, nothing doing. Pathfinders, yes; anything else, yes; but 617, no. Do you know they fly so low you can't even let out your trailing aerial?'

Yes, that was just the point. No more oxygen masks; no more piling on of heavy clothing; no more heavy flak; no more of that nasty dizzy feeling when peering over the side from 16,000 feet. Just trees and chimneys and occasional bursts of light flak—and even not that if one succeeded in keeping down close enough to the deck. What stirring visions of success and victory went racing through my mind as I called in at Group Headquarters to report to the A.O.C. and collect my orders.

Sir Ralph Cochrane, however, was well equipped to deal with just this situation. First he informed me that the Squadron had changed its role. Henceforth high flying, not low, was the order of the day—to be precise, 20,000 feet. There was a special target in sight, and a special bomb to attack it which would have to penetrate very deep and therefore be dropped from very high. Did I like high flying? No? Well, that was a pity, because I would get plenty of it, until I could guarantee one fifteen-yard error out of three bombs from 20,000 feet. And perhaps I would give some thought to the question of marking, because the target wouldn't be visible from 20,000 feet at night; someone would have to mark it.

Ah, yes, so they would.

But Sir Ralph had noticed the gleam in my eye.

'I don't want you to get any false ideas on that score. The marking is not to be done low level. Low level doesn't pay; we've already lost three-quarters of the Squadron because of it, and it's not to be repeated unless there's another dam to attack. I want the marking done scientifically, using modern instruments; and that means high up.'

So that was that; there was nothing to be said or argued.

Then he sent me to Balderton for a conversion course on to Lancasters. I, who had done four tours of operations and two as an instructor! I, who when the Squadron had been re-equipped with Halifaxes, the most unmanageable four-engined aircraft in the Service, had not been given so much as an hour of dual, but merely told to get on with it! That after all this, and much else besides, *I* should be sent back to school as a pupil.

But the A.O.C. was immovable. The interview, he intimated, was over; there was a car waiting at the door; I could go. And the harder I worked the sooner I'd be out.

When I finally reached Connigsby I found the rest of the Squadron in much the same frame of mind as myself. They were fed up, browned off, ready to mutiny if Group didn't put an end to the bombing practices and give them an operation. Neither did they see why they should have to accept a C.O. from outside their own ranks. And who could blame them? On walking out of the Accounts Section—which even an ex-Group Captain must pay his respects to if he wants to draw any pay (and then only in the Treasury's good time)—a station-wagon flashed by with two Flight Lieutenants inside. One was small and had a face like a cherub; the other was large and had a neck like a bulldog. They both turned round in their seats, in perfect formation, looked at me as if to say 'My God, what next,' and drove on with redoubled speed.

Nor did the remaining three months of the year do anything to help. For in place of the action for which we had forgone our ranks and our pay, there was nothing but high-level bombing schedules on Wainfleet ranges. Just bombing by day, and bombing by night; month after month. Not any sort of bombing, but planned and calculated down to the nearest ten feet of altitude, the nearest mile per hour, the nearest ten seconds of timing. A bombing run that started twenty-five miles short of the target and carried on steadily as a rock, neither five feet up nor down, neither half a knot faster or slower, with neither thought for flak nor fighter. From the bomb-aimer a mechanical, tuneless monologue:

'Steady.... Steady ... much steadier than that. ... Right

.... right a little. Steady. Steady. . . . No, no good. . . . Bomb-doors closed; come in again. . . .'

Over and over again.

And when back on the Station, charts to prepare, averages to work out, explanations to give, new instructions to be followed, discussions as to how to drop a marker within fifteen yards without coming lower than 5,000 feet. No wonder there were deputations to the Station Commander, to Group Headquarters, to the A.O.C. himself; and petitions to the Squadron Commander by the score, in the office, in the hangars, over the intercom, in the bar. But the A.O.C. was adamant as rock; he yielded not an inch:

'Bring the Squadron average down to fifty yards and solve the marking problem. Then you can go. Only then. . . . Low flying? Yes, you are still officially a low-flying squadron; you can keep up your schedules. But only as a training exercise.'

And so we did.

We flew in fine weather and in bad, in moonlight and in half moonlight; sometimes on our own, sometimes in flights of three, sometimes in full squadron formation; but always very low, until the Mess began to fill up with relics and trophies—with grass and hay sucked up into the air intakes, telephone wires wound round the propellers, and occasional twigs and branches. To those who thought they already knew how to fly low it was a startling revelation, sometimes more than a revelation—a bringing down to earth with an almighty bump. But mercifully only once a fatal one. Such flying as this was not without its effect on those who took part. Indeed, how could it be otherwise? Who could fail to respond to the magic of the moon-swept, fairylike countryside disappearing so effortlessly a few feet beneath the nose? And what of the bomb-aimer out in front, with nothing but perspex between himself and the onrushing scenery? What must not be his feelings, wondering how the pilot is standing up to it, whether his hand is growing tired, or his eye sleepy; deliberating whether perhaps it is not time, this once at least, to give a warning shout. Such a tall line of chimneys; so many and so close together; for making bricks—or is it tombstones? Getting so close. Closer. Even closer. Too late. TOO LATE. Aaah. Of course, how stupid. Not over the top, but in between, with a last-minute dip of the wing to slip through the gap. But, phew, what a horrible sinking feeling in the pit of the stomach; what an uncomfortable lurch as the port wing drops and top rudder keeps the wing-tip from hitting the ground.

Yes, no wonder things were liable to go to a bomb-aimer's head, especially if he should happen to be an Australian sheep farmer used to the wide-open backlocks of Victoria and to being answerable to none but himself, as was Keith Astbury, whom they entrusted to me. No wonder the pilots should find a new stimulus to their imagination, especially those who had burst the dams and survived the Dortmund Ems, like Joe McCarthy, the thick-set American from Brooklyn, or Les Munro the stolid New Zealand farmer, or Mick Martin the thin, at times scraggy-looking, Australian, perhaps the greatest operational low flyer of all time, or Dave Shannon, his impossibly young-looking compatriot. No wonder there should begin to appear signs of a concerted plot to break the ban on low-level marking. No wonder Group should post us away to an aerodrome all of our own, Woodhall Spa, where no one could see or hear what was going on, what schemes were being hatched, what the training and planning was all about.

And indeed what was it all about? We were not long in finding out. Across the Channel, in the Pas de Calais, were being massed gang upon gang of forced labourers who were feverishly digging, excavating, burrowing; and not content with that were pouring ton upon ton of concrete into the holes they made. At first they were watched with interest, mixed perhaps with pity for men who had to work so incessantly and so hard. But before long the interest changed to concern, almost alarm. From the shores of the Baltic came reports of a new weapon; not a V1, or even a V2, but a V3, a gigantic gun designed to fire two 500 lb. shells a minute into London. What if the gun should prove successful? What if it should be mounted in these underground fortresses, where beneath fifty feet of reinforced concrete and more no bomb could hope to reach them? What would become of London then? Poor London, the pride of the whole world, already the victim of so many attacks. And the seat of the Government, too. Yes, the Government. Just think if something should happen to the Government. No, at all costs London must be protected, even, if it comes to a pinch, at the cost of raising a ban on low-level marking.

And so the day came when Sir Ralph issued a new directive:

'You've got one chance. Just one, and you stand or fall by it. The target is the Gnome-Rhône aero-engine factory at Limoges. But it is in a built-up area, and there are 500 girls on night shift. You are to destroy the factory, but not take a single life inside it or outside. That's a direct instruction from the War Cabinet. If you fail you'll never get another chance; but if you succeed . . . well, wait and see.'

The attack was scheduled for the full-moon period of February and went without a hitch. From the French coast onwards there was a thin layer of stratus, sufficient to make us bring the main force down below it, but not sufficient to obscure the light of the moon. At zero minus ten Mick dropped the orbiting marker twenty-five miles to the north-east, while we ourselves did three low-level runs over the target, firing our guns into the air as a warning to the girls to get out. At zero minus two we dropped the first load of target markers from point-blank range. The rear gunner thought they had bounced and hit our tail. But they hadn't; it was just that we were unusually low. Once we had checked that they were where they should be and had received confirmation from Mick, we ordered the main force in. First Shannon. Next Munro. Next McCarthy. Then the others. As each bomb fell it was checked for accuracy before permission was given for the next. The seventh missed by thirty yards and fell in the river due to the marker becoming obscured by smoke. So Mick dropped a second load of markers, and the remaining bombs were ordered in—all in all ten 12,000 pounders in a factory 200 yards long by 100 yards wide. We signalled home 'Mission complete', and at the request of Kelly, who sat throughout the attack with his nose glued to the navigation table, circled round the city twice, wondering how many days off work the girls would be given, and whether or not they would drink our health. When photographic reconnaissance revealed a completely flattened target, and the Resistance reported that there had been no loss of life and only one injury (and this because the girl refused to go farther than the ditch outside the gates), the War Cabinet sent us a personal message of congratulations. We were off.

For the next two months targets followed one another in rapid succession. At Clermont-Ferrand we destroyed the two main sheds of the Michelin rubber factory, without touching the canteen sandwiched between them. At La Ricamarie, a minute ball-bearing factory hidden in the haze of an industrial valley with steep hills on either side, my own markers, dropped on the seventh run in, landed a hundred yards short, and Dave's bounced off the roof to land 150 yards beyond. We kept up the attack for an hour and forty minutes before giving it up as a bad job, but fortune was on our side, for subsequent reconnaissance showed the target obliterated, though sad to tell some of the neighbouring houses too.

At Angoulême we blew up the powder factory with an explosion larger even than Wilhelmshaven; and at Bergerac we repeated the performance to greater effect still.

But at Antheor, on the shores of the Mediterranean, we failed. The target was the smallest we had yet been given, a viaduct carrying the main railway communications from Italy. The Americans had bombed it; the Navy shelled it; now it was up to us. One 12,000 lb. bomb within fifteen yards, they said, would do it. Well, judging from past records, that should be easy enough; and even if the defences, as reported, were heavier than anything we had met before, a quick break through and out should amply do the trick. But from the very beginning we ran into trouble. On the way down to advanced base I myself lost an engine and was forced to take Joe McCarthy's precious Q for Queenie, Number 3 marker and the apple of his eyes. That only left Mick and ourselves to do the marking. It also left an infuriated and desperate Joe, who had interrupted his leave in order to take part in the attack, and had never missed an operation. At zero minus five, when the coastline loomed in sight with the Bay of Antheor twenty degrees away to port, the mountains looked so formidable that instead of diving head-on down the gorge, I began to circle, hoping for an easier line of approach. It was then that the flak opened up, very heavy and accurate. After two abortive attempts to come in parallel with the mountains, and while still juggling for an opening, Mick called up to say that he was in position running down the gorge, and please to keep the flak engaged for another thirty seconds. Considering the strength of the opposition and the sheer drop of the mountains it was a staggering performance for a heavy bomber.

But 2,000 yards short of the target the searchlights caught him, and a battery of 88 mm., based on the viaduct itself, opened up. It was point-blank range over open sights, and a semi-circle of firemen pumping water into a solitary bonfire could hardly have had an easier task.

'My God, he'll never get through!'

It was Astbury, from the nose.

But on he came, straight as a die, hugging the mountainside, drenched in a veritable torrent of tracer. To us sitting over the top, no longer conscious of the shells bursting around us, the thirty seconds might as well have been as many minutes or hours.

Then suddenly the tracer stopped. Not a single flicker, not a sign of life.

'Fourteen, fifteen . . . sixteen. . . .'

32

Kelly was counting in a kind of Shakespearian voice. But he was rudely interrupted as the tracer and the search-lights opened up once again—only now in reverse, out to sea.

So Mick had made it. He was over the viaduct and racing for safety.

'Twenty . . . twenty-one . . . twenty-two.'

And still the guns were firing—from port, from starboard, from astern, from the quarter, from above, from everywhere except below; intersecting, one would say, inside the cockpit itself. Would it never end? Would the bullets go on missing for ever? Or was the plane just a ghost, transparent and intangible, and the scene just a passing fancy?

'Twenty-three . . . twenty-four . . . twenty-four.'

The tracer was faltering. Faltering.

'Twenty-five . . . twenty-five . . . twenty-five it is.'

From somewhere inside the aircraft there was a long sigh. Below, just a Mediterranean coastline bathed in moonlight. Outside, the thump and roar of bursting shells, hitherto un-noticed, but now gradually reasserting themselves.

'Something's happened, sir. There are no markers on the viaduct. And Mick wouldn't have gone slap over the top with-out having a shot, not even in the face of that lot.'

That was true. He wouldn't; not Mick.

'Wait a minute, Keith; there's a message coming through, so faint I can hardly hear. Keep quiet and listen. For God's sake listen.'

I let go of the stick and pressed the earphones into my ears. But even so it was so faint. So fearfully faint.

'We're hit . . . Bob . . . through the head. . . . Just about to press button. . . . Can't make it home.'

So that was it. Bob Hay killed, and just at the last moment, too late for Mick to take over and press the bomb-release him-self. Bob Hay, Mick's best friend. But if he couldn't get back over the mountains and through the flak, then he couldn't get to North Africa either, for that was even farther still, and we weren't carrying Mediterranean maps. Then what, for heaven's sake, was the alternative?

'Making . . . Corsica. . . .'

Ah, Corsica. Yes, of course. Wherever that might be—and in whoever's hands. Still, no use worrying or asking unnecessary questions. Mick must know what he was doing. But stop, another message. So faint. Too faint to catch. But one must. One positively must. It might be a matter of life and death.

'Sorry sir, about the markers. Very sorry.'

Ah, you're sorry, Mick. Then, my God, what of me?

But I'll learn, Mick. At least I can promise you that. I'll remember that an opportunity missed is missed for ever, and come what may I'll never hesitate again, at least not once I've caught sight of the target. So help me God.

Antheor proved a costly operation indeed. It lost us Mick, who on his eventual return from Corsica was posted for a rest to night intruders; it lost us Q for Queenie, which on inspection was so heavily damaged as to be categorized as a complete write-off; it lost us one of the new crews, who flew into a hill in cloud; it failed to destroy the viaduct, in spite of one bomb twenty yards from the aiming-point. Worse still, it threatened the whole future of the low-level marking technique, for if the defences of Antheor were enough to stop us, then what of Germany itself?

But unknown to us Sir Ralph had wider horizons in view even than the destruction of V3's, and he had already made up his mind. He sent word to say that the Commander-in-Chief was offering four Mosquitoes as marker aircraft on condition that we proved the worth of the technique by marking Munich, the heaviest defended target outside Berlin. Were we game for the challenge?

Were we!

But as things turned out, we did not have an easy run. In the first place we were hardly given time to familiarize ourselves on the aircraft. In the second we were sent off before the arrival of the auxiliary drop-tanks, and without these, even allowing for take-off from the nearest point on the English coast, and assuming that one remained on track from start to finish and spent only two minutes on target, we couldn't hope for more than thirteen minutes' petrol on returning to base. In the navigation room Danny Walker and the others looked as if they were on the verge of mutiny, but there was nothing to be done. We lined the Mosquitoes up on the down-wind end of the runway, filled them to overflowing, and took off the moment the oil temperature needle began to move. Beside me in the navigator's seat Pat Kelly remained unusually quiet, hunched up over his maps as if searching for some long-lost secret. The winds were high, and the weather hostile. A few miles short of Karlsruhe, whose defences we could not afford to circumvent, there came a faint, but familiar, voice on V.H.F.

'Anything cooking, sir?' Then a loud guffaw. It was Mick. But what on earth could Mick be doing so far afield, and on this night of all nights! Even Kelly's weatherbeaten Manxman's features showed a trace of emotion.

'A little bird . . . a little bird told me something interesting . . . we're on the prowl. Just prowling around . . . just in case . . . that's all, sir . . . but see you don't miss. . . . It wouldn't do to miss.'

No, that at least was certain; we wouldn't miss. Not now that the team was complete once again.

'Boy, that's something, isn't it? That will show 'em that it doesn't pay to mess around, not with us. Another forty-nine minutes; that's all. Then they'll know what it's all about.'

Pat thrust his pencil inside his tight-fitting helmet and relaxed for the first time since briefing at midday.

'The way we're going, I reckon we'll get home with twelve minutes to spare—provided, that is, you don't spend more than sixty seconds on target.'

At zero hour precisely, as we sailed into the target area, the flare force dropped their flares, stick upon stick of them.

Down on the port side lay the railway station, its curved roofs gleaming unmistakably in the bright flare light. I ran my eye eastwards in line with the railway track to pick up the aiming-point. It was easy enough to find—the large block that served as the Gestapo Headquarters.

Who could ask for anything more deserving of being destroyed?

But wait! We have mistimed it by a fraction, and are almost over the top, far too close to start the dive. It would mean going down almost vertically; and that would lead to exceeding the speed safety factor. It would mean that the bombs would foul the forward bulkhead. And what then? No, out a little and haul off so as to get a run at it. But wait; can we afford to? A minute to get back into position—anyway, forty-five seconds. And we've only got sixty to spare. And suppose the flares go out? Or drift away from the aiming-point? Or we lose sight of the aiming-point at the turn? Things seem to be hotting up somewhat too—to use a polite kind of phrase. No, that won't do; it's now or never. Pretend you're a cormorant; *they* don't mess around once they see a fish. Pull the nose up; right up. Up. I know you're not fond of aero-batics, but this isn't aerobatics; it's sheer necessity. That's it. Now over on the port wing-tip and down. Down. Down. What a curious floating feeling. And what's that map doing up there on the windshield? Get it out of the way, Pat, and never mind about calling out the seconds. I know there's sixty in all and that ten have gone already. But I've got to keep my eye on that rotten building, and there's enough to do, what with opening bomb-doors, missing those blasted flares, squint-ing through the searchlights, lining up on the target and judging our height, without trying to look through a some-thing, something map. Ah, that's better. There she is. Just look at her; a sitting duck. Coming up so nicely, so nicely. Vertically beneath us—or almost. Which means that the bombs will almost certainly foul the bulkhead. I wonder what will happen when they do? And the speed. The book says 'Not to exceed 400 m.p.h.' Well, we reached that some time ago, and we're way off the clock now: but everything's happening too fast to work it all out, and nothing matters so long as that target stays put in the gunsight. Two seconds more and I think that will do it. Yes, it will have to; it's looming up very fast. Too fast. Pull back on the stick, and press the button; that will throw the bombs clear. Ah, it has. Atta-boy! But the pull-out. What about the pull-out? Misjudged it. Much too steep and much too low. Pull back, as hard as you can. Harder. Harder. Wonder if this is what a fighter-pilot does? Everything's going dim. Even old Kelly's stopped nattering about the time. Won't it be funny if we don't make it? Everyone will say we were shot down, when in point of fact it was only a bit of bad judgement, the sort of thing a sprog pilot gets an endorsement for—or would do if he survived.

My God, now where are we? There're lights through the windscreen, lights through the canopy, lights down between the engine nacelles, and the target seems to be high up through the starboard window. Does that mean we're upside down? And if so, what's the procedure for recovery? That's something the A.O.C. never included in his rotten conversion course—still, he does know what he wants, he *did* get us Mosquitoes, and the admin. staff are scared stiff of him, which is a jolly healthy sign. No, we won't let him down tonight. But just for the moment we're in a terrible mess; if only somebody could only do something. Anything; no matter what it is. Pat, can't you suggest something instead of sitting there like a cabbage?

'Thirty seconds.'

Thirty seconds. Is it only twenty then since the whole thing started? No, surely not, it must be a mistake. We've been ages. Ages and ages. Hullo, that's peculiar, the target's suddenly appeared on the port side. And there are the markers, burning so brightly. Just half a moment and I'll get my orientation. That's it, they're there. They're there. Inside the square, 150 yards east of the railway station. Anyway, as near as damn it, and we're not worrying about inches tonight. Now call up the rest of the marker force and get on with it. In you come, Dave, straight in and out, and the rest of you too. No circling, no identifying, just in and the hell out of it. And what about you up top, Les? Are you ready to back up? Well, stand by to start. They're turning on the heat good and proper and the quicker everyone gets out the better, so long as they don't rush the bombing run. We haven't come through all this just to plaster the daisies. What's that on the other side of the river? It's a load of markers, but who on earth went and dropped them there? And they're attracting the bombing. Les, for God's sake cancel them; drop a stick of green markers on top and call up the Main Force and warn them off. And for heaven's sake don't miss. It must be one of the Marker Force shot down, markers and all; and he's landed just close enough to make people think it's the aiming-point. I wonder who. But no, I mustn't block the air finding out that, and we'll have to get moving.

Yes, my God, we will too. Pat's making a terrible scene bawling out that we've had it, that we're four minutes over-due, and I don't know what else. Not printable most of it. And come to think of it, now that all our markers are gone, there's not much else we can do—except have a look. But it's worth having a look at, isn't it? How well it's going. Almost too well to be true. If it hadn't been for that accidental load of markers it would have been 100 per cent. And now it's all over bar the shouting. Or is it? What's that thud? Thud. Thud. Might almost be Antheor all over again. Pat, what is it? Yes, I know it sounds like flak, but I don't believe it. We're 1,500 feet and clocking 300 plus. No heavy flak in the world can follow at that height and speed. But you're right, it *is* flak. And it has caught us up too; in front of us; beside us, all round us. It hangs on like a leech no matter how much evasive action we take; hangs on like a leech. Pat, give me a new course; I think I must have veered round back into the defences, for we ought to have been clear minutes ago, and they're still hitting us.

Pat, stop swearing. Get me a pinpoint, and give me the quickest course out of this filthy muck. No, cancel that, don't stop swearing; keep it up, it does me good. It gets a great load off my chest. I don't mind getting shot up over the target or going into the target or even leaving the target, but once I've said to myself, 'Ah, we're out of it now and in the clear', then my defences are down; I've got nothing left to fight back with. Or, anyway, so it seems. For God's sake, is it never going to stop? Is it going to follow us all the way home? No, not all the way; just the first eight minutes, and the last two. For sitting over the top of Manston was an enemy fighter, and he almost got us as we were coming in to land. But not quite. No, not quite.

Munich made up for all the trials of the past, and a good deal more. It won the Squadron a week's stand-down and leave; it gave us our Mosquitoes and two Pathfinder squadrons into the bargain to back us up; it inflicted damage that was estimated at forty times as much as the combined Anglo-American attacks of the last three years. Above all, it marked the end of our period of probation and the beginning of our life of action. And how varied and full this life was to be. How well it suited the crews. How surely and steadily it marched on towards its climax.

And how swiftly that climax came to a head.

Around the middle of June, less than a fortnight after the Normandy landings, the order came to stand by for our great offensive. By this time Wallis' deep penetration bomb, Tallboy, had arrived on the Station and been tried and tested. It had dug a seventy-foot-deep hole at the mouth of the Saumur railway tunnel and caved in the roof fifty yards inside the tunnel itself. It had smashed the hitherto impregnable U-boat pens at Le Havre and Boulogne, sunk the forty or so E-boats lying in the harbours, and blown at least two of them clean out of the water on to the wharf itself. So outstanding had been its power of penetration and its accuracy that a whole new series of targets were brought within the Squadron's orbit, and only shortage of time prevented our dealing with them all. For the V3's were reported ready to fire; and it was now or never.

But as luck would have it, no sooner were we given our orders than ten-tenths cloud descended on the whole of the Pas de Calais. Such urgency did the Cabinet attach to the protection of London—or, as some people said, to that of the Government—that we were held on instant readiness to go either by day or by night whenever the weather should clear. Four days later we were still sitting up at Flights, having slept there, eaten up there, gambled up there, grumbled up there, and heavens knows what else. The weight of the bombs plus the petrol load had proved too heavy for the undercarriages, and the emergency was only met by keeping the entire ground crews on a non-stop rota of bombing-up and un-bombing, fuelling and de-fuelling in such a way that no one aircraft ever stood more than four hours fully loaded, and yet that all could take off at two hours' notice. With ordinary bombs it would have been simple enough, but Wallis's 12,000 lb. Tall-boy, streamlined like a rocket and polished like a mirror to gain every ounce of speed, required a gang of six qualified armourers, and a special bombing-up trolley, of which we only had two. Life was by no means easy.

In between the fuss and bother, the moaning and the groaning, when time began to hang heavy, a new topic of conversation was raised. What would we do when the war was won—as by the looks of things it soon would be? The suggestions ranged from the near sublime to the half ridiculous —from a crusade to end war for all time to a volunteer shock squadron in China; from a private air network in the Bahamas to a global blitz on politicians and their empty promises. But through all the discussion there ran two common themes— adventure and teamwork. If adventure was to go, peace would not be worth having; if teamwork was to go, there would be no peace at all. We on our part would do our best to see to it that this peace was not like the last one; that instead of a wild stampede, each man for himself, there would remain the spirit of the operational squadrons—of all three Services; a spirit of duty first, of all in the same boat pulling the same way, acknowledging no rest until the victory be won; above all, that those who had laid down their lives would not be forgotten.

On the morning of the fifth day a top priority message came through to say that the weather was deteriorating still further and that we could stand down for twenty-four hours, but were to stay in the Mess. The Station Commander said: 'Ah, that's good; now I can attend the Group Savings Certificate Conference.' McCarthy and Munro said nothing, but slunk off unseen to a pub at Boston. The ground crews set about de-bombing and de-fuelling. Everyone else retired to the Mess as per instructions.

Phew, what a relief. A bath to soak in. A table to eat off. A bar to lean against. Nothing to worry about.

Two hours later a second message came through; the weather had cleared; we were on target at four o'clock.

Typical Met! Absolutely typical!

But, my God, four o'clock. Do they know what they are asking? Allow three hours for take-off, climbing to height and flight into the target area; that makes one o'clock. It's now twelve. That leaves one hour to warn the crews, reverse the de-bombing and de-fuelling, work out the flight plan, brief, contact Fighter Command (through a non-existent channel of communications), get something to eat and into the aircraft. They're mad. And as if half an hour, or even one hour would make the slightest difference. Ring them up and tell them what you think of them. A golden opportunity. No, don't do that. Never let it be said that 617 couldn't cope. And, anyway, they're only administrators; one mustn't be too hard on them.

McCarthy? Well, what about him? Disappeared? Munro too? My God, we're going in formation; Munro's in the lead and Mac's number two. Find them. Go out and get them.

Ring up every pub in town. Send out a search-party. I don't mind who goes, what speed-limits he breaks, what lights he jumps, what state of nerves they all come back in. But they've got to be sitting in their aircraft forty-four minutes from now, all of them. And declare a state of emergency. The Station Master's not here; he's arguing Savings campaigns. Do it yourself. Pull the W.A.A.F.s out of the telephone exchange and put them on duty up at Flights. It will make the men work faster, and the fewer telephone calls there are, the better. Bomb-aimers, engineers, gunners—eat. Pilots and navigators, up to Flights. Cancel all calls on transport and mobilize the lot for squadron duty.

Ah, here's the Station Commander back. Sooner than I expected. But at least he looks calm and collected. A bit solemn, perhaps; but still, not in a flap. That's one up to him.

'Cheshire, I want to speak to you in my office.'

In his office! But I haven't even time to get anything to eat. How can I drive over to his office?

'This is no time to try and be funny.'

No, indeed.

'I don't often interfere with your plans, but this time I insist. It's a very serious situation. If you refuse to come to my office, come outside. I'll talk to you there.'

My God, have the guns started firing? Have we missed the boat? Has there been an unexpected development across the Channel? But why can't he just come out with it here and now? Can't we dispense with formality, just this once?

'I'm extremely sorry to have to say it, but 617 has let me down badly, very badly. It's bottom of the Savings ladder.'

You don't say. You—— But no; hold on! One mustn't let oneself go, not even with a madman. And, anyway, the odds are that he's so much up in the clouds with all this Savings campaign that he still hasn't cottoned on to what's happening. But he'll have to find out from someone else. If I tell him he'll start asking a hundred and one questions. And I simply can't stand it. Not at this juncture. I'll just accept the rebuke and go.

42

Ah, what's this? A station-wagon. Half out of control, by the look of it. It must be Munro and McCarthy. Yes, it is. That will divert him. For it isn't every day of the year that he watches two senior Flight Commanders come screaming broadside across a 'Stop, look and listen before you cross' area, and then leap out in front of his nose like a pair of runaway bandits without so much as a nod or a salute.

'Back into that brake, Les, and out to the aircraft. Your helmet's there; your 'chute's there; and you'll be briefed in flight. You're airborne in three minutes. Three minutes. In your usual role. Number 1. And you'll hear the rest when you get back.'

Yes, when you get back. But you so nearly didn't. You made four runs into the target, one to drop your own bomb and three to draw the flak from others who were running in to drop theirs. How awe-inspiring it all looked from the Mosquito 12,000 feet below you, watching you shrouded in a canopy of shell-bursts, and each run so steady, so slow, so long—seven minutes a time—thinking that every half-second must be your last. And yet it wasn't. Others came down out of the sky, but you didn't. It must be that New Zealand doggedness which makes you so determined to see a thing through once it's started, like that night you lost an engine 100 feet after take-off, and carried on all the way to the target because you were put in charge of the bombing force and felt it was your duty. And now you've reaped your reward; you've watched each of the five new sites pulverized out of action.

They'll never fire on London now. Other weapons may, but not these—if, of course, they ever would have done, for Intelligence officers aren't exactly infallible. But anyway, that's not your concern; yours was just to go and do as you were told. And now, almost before we've begun, it's all over. The A.O.C.'s posted us. Lock, stock, and barrel—all the old hands, that is. It's no use arguing with him; I've tried that before. We've just got to grin and bear it.

Grin. It's funny I should say that, because we always used to call you Happy on account of the fact that you grinned so seldom. But now that the shock of posting has worn off you're grinning all over your face. And so are Dave and Mac. All like a bunch of schoolchildren. And I suppose I am too. Even Vicky, who can smile just as well as any human being, has a boyish glint in his eye that I've never noticed before. Willy Tait's coming this afternoon to take over the Squadron; and we'll make him grin too. Everybody will grin. Which reminds me that I have an old score to pay off. Willy turned me upside down on the way back from York. Now I'm going to do the same thing to him; not through a car roof, but head first from the top of the bar, minus his trousers and essential underwear.

And there's something else I have to do. I must go to the A.O.C. and tell him that it was that rotten conversion course of his which pulled me through it all. It rankled at the time, but that's over now. Deep down inside me I know that it pays to be taught by those who know.

3

SUMMER 1945, Washington D.C. The doldrums. Not a
breath of wind from any quarter. Not a ripple on the
surface of the water. Not the remotest sign of hope on
the horizon. Just drift, drift, drift. Get up at 8.15; breakfast
8.45; drive to the office of the British Joint Staff Mission—
one-way traffic all the way in. Go through files until 12.30;
lunch in the canteen; more files till 5; then get picked up on
Constitution Avenue—one-way traffic all the way back. After
that, house decorating, or move the furniture around, or go
to a party, or just sit and talk. Occasionally a trip in the
Beechcraft to Florida or the Bahamas or Toronto to let off
steam and to justify my job, but all so far removed from the
winning of the war, and so seemingly pointless.

Small wonder that under such conditions as these there
should be inward murmuring and discord; mutiny of the crew
against the Captain for having steered the ship into such an
impasse; discontent of the Captain against all and sundry for
not having prevented it happening. Some of the crew pressing
for a return to operational flying whatever the cost, almost
whatever the means; others leapfrogging the war and looking
for some great and glorious career to follow on; perhaps the
conquest of space; perhaps the champion of the underdog,
wherever he might be; perhaps a chain of radio stations linking
the ordinary people of the world together in the cause of peace
and understanding. Anything, so long as there was something

to throw oneself into body and soul, something truly worth living for, and even if need be worth dying for. But on the other side of the balance the duties of married life, the claims of Constance, whose heart was in America and in the hope of a period of peace and security. And so a hard-won compromise was reached—settle down in Mexico or in the South Sea Islands, or some such place where everything was full of beauty and glamour, and set about changing the world through the instrument of the pen.

The pen! On the face of things a most commonplace and valueless instrument, but according to those who ought to know, the most powerful weapon in the world, mightier than the sword and the low-level bomber, mightier even than a chain of radio stations or a fleet of space ships, mighty enough to conquer nations, to change the course of history and to earn oneself a fortune. Just imagine. Ah, just imagine! But unfortunately the imagination was not to be tempted. It could foresee hard work, hours of drudgery and disappointments; it visualized reading polite letters from publishers, sitting in the waiting-rooms of agents' offices, invoking the help of chance and influential acquaintances, but it conjured up no stimulating visions of immediate success and fame, no pictures of a breathless world waiting impatiently for the next masterpiece; nothing but an endless rut, becoming ever deeper, deeper, deeper. Then, just to settle the issue once and for all, came the news of the end of the German war. All was now over bar the shouting. The last lingering hope of some unforeseen crisis that would lead to a recall to one of the battle-fronts was crushed. So far as the eye could see the doldrums reigned supreme. Not a breath, not a movement from sea or heaven. Even Washington itself was boiling up for a heatwave.

Then came the sudden flying visit to England to welcome Christopher home from prison camp, and the unexpected development in the Vanity Fair.

It was late at night—the third of an almost non-stop

celebration. Christopher himself had retired to bed, feeling, no doubt, the strain of his four years behind barbed wire, and the original party had dwindled to a mere three or four, most of them regulars of the Mayfair round. Suddenly the conversation turned to religion.

Religion! In the Vanity Fair! And from those who spent more of their time drinking gin than anything else! The situation was so fantastic that I burst out laughing. But even this did not deter them, and so eloquent and voluble did they become, attracting more and more attention from the bar, that I all but regretted having not followed Christopher's example and gone back home to the Ritz. Then finally the most voluble of them all leant across the table at me and asked:

'How much do you know about God?'

She was a good-looking girl, whom I had met only twice before, a trifle worn perhaps from too many late nights and too much gin, but not the sort to fall for religion nor to lose her balance for more than a passing moment. So I answered in no uncertain terms—for her own good as much as to put an end to a futile conversation:

'God is an inward conscience, personal to us all, that tells us what we ought to do and what we ought not; one thing to some of us, another to others. It's just as simple as that, and if only people wouldn't go and confuse the issue by bringing religion into it, the world would be a lot better off.'

'Absolute nonsense. God is a person. A PERSON. And you know it just as well as I do. You ought to be ashamed of yourself.'

If ever there was an occasion for bursting out laughing, it was now. But I didn't laugh. I couldn't. For I suddenly knew that what she had said was true. God really was a person. It wasn't that I had known it subconsciously all along and merely needed a jolt to bring it out into the open; nor that I had followed the arguments step by step and found them unanswerable; but purely and simply that I knew. God *was* a person. I *was* slightly ashamed. Nor was this all. For now I knew that

47

I would have to get up and do something about—not IT; but HIM; that to take Him into account just on Sundays or even at intervals during the week would not be enough; that henceforth it must be either all or nothing.

But then there broke in a further thought—a very sobering one. The clergy. Their way of speaking; their teaching; their do's and their don'ts. Was I prepared to commit myself to all this? No, I wasn't. Anyway, not on the spur of the moment. Better for the time being to sit on the fence.

Back in Washington, where I found myself a few days later, life was never to resume the old routine. Hardly had I taken stock of the files in the in-tray when I was sent for by Field Marshal Lord Maitland Wilson. According to those who knew, the only other occasion on which an R.A.F. officer below air rank had been sent for by the Army Commander was prior to his being cashiered, and it was not without some enquiring looks and uplifted eyebrows that I duly answered the summons. The arrangement of the Field Marshal's headquarters did little to help. I started off in an office staffed by some female secretaries and a Lieutenant. From there I was ushered somewhat formally into another office where the ranks were considerably more senior, and finally with yet more formality into the Holy of Holies itself, the floor of which appeared to take several minutes to cross. Lord Maitland Wilson, whose proportions were of no mean size when seen from a distance, unexpectedly rose from his chair and shook me warmly by the hand. He invited me to sit down and said that the Allies had invented an atom bomb.

Just like that.

Admittedly the subject was not entirely new, for it had cropped up in one of our conferences on space travel when a learned-looking scientist had informed us that one day science would succeed in harnessing atomic energy, and that would mean the revolutionizing of rocket propulsion, and the end of the oil industry. None the less, the news came like a bolt from the blue. A shattering bolt, too. The Field Marshal asked if I had any knowledge of physics, and looked decidedly relieved when I told him that I had not. Then he proceeded to tell me what an atomic bomb was, much as one might expect a cadet to do when suddenly called upon to explain Einstein's Theory of Relativity to his class-mates. Once he had assured himself that I was not in a position to ask any technical questions, he said that the bomb was to be dropped on Japan in the hope that it would finish off the war without the necessity of an invasion. An invasion, as I could well imagine, would lead to far greater casualties on both sides than one, or even half a dozen, atom bombs, and therefore there was enough justification for dropping the bomb.

Although the bomb had been built in America and was to be dropped by the U.S.A.A.F., it was England who had done the initial research and shown how to set about it, and therefore two British observers were to take part in the attack. One was to be William Penney, a scientist who knew more about the bomb than anyone else living, and the other was to be myself. It was his job to look after the technical aspect, and mine to report on the tactical problems involved in getting the bomb on to the target. After going into a few final details, he poised two enormous hands a foot or two above his desk, and explained that the bomb would be exploded 1,000 feet above the ground in such a way that the blast effect would be at its greatest and pulverize everything beneath it. As he finished speaking, he dropped his hands on to the blotter, much as an elephant might stamp on the wooden deck of a ship, and held them there until the pens, inkstand, blotter, and all the rest had returned to their normal static position. I now understood why he had been given the nickname 'Jumbo'.

There followed three difficult weeks of marking time, of being briefed more closely on what was expected of me, and of unsuccessfully trying to look as if nothing unusual had happened in the Field Marshal's office. Then my marching orders came through, and I was processed through Hamilton

Field, San Francisco, for the Mid-Pacific. Whoever has been through the same experience, transmuted as it were into a parcel and consigned to the charge of the postal authorities second class air mail, will understand the significance of the word 'processed'. He will also understand how, having been shorn of all individuality and reduced to the status of an automaton, his mind is liable to start racing. This is what mine did. It raced and raced until it was fit to seize up solid. It raced not merely across the five continents, not merely under the Seven Seas, not merely through the utmost reaches of the upper atmosphere, but round the very circumference of the moon itself, finally coming to rest in the House of Commons. There, before the most crowded gallery known to history, it conjured up a picture of so stirring and dramatic a speech that the very chroniclers themselves were at a loss to know how to record it and the listeners in the galleries rose to their feet vowing to dedicate the rest of their lives to the cause of peace amongst nations. So vivid was the picture that I could hardly wait to return to England and unleash myself upon whoever would listen.

By way of distraction, when the machinery felt as if it were in need of lubrication, I turned to a book that I had been given that night in the Vanity Fair. It went by the curious name of *Screwtape Letters*, and from what I could make out was a kind of textbook for young Devils written by their Commander-in-Chief. It was all a good deal beyond my comprehension, to say the least, but as I read I felt stirring within me an uneasiness. I began to wonder whether there was not perhaps more to life than the things one could see and touch and calculate on a slide-rule.

I was not allowed to wonder for long. After a week or two's preparation on the island base of Tinian, we took off on our long-awaited flight. Three days previously Hiroshima had been destroyed, and the Japanese had not surrendered. Now it was time to launch another attack. To Bill Penney, doing his first operational flight, it must have been a strange experience. But to me, doing my last, it was stranger still. We started off by sitting through an interminable briefing; we boarded our planes in the glare of arc lights and the whirr of movie cameras; we were briefed to fly at 30,000 feet but flew at 39,000, where it would be 'safer'; we were far out of range of flak and fighter, but took evasive action at the least provocation. Explicable, no doubt, by the singularity of the occasion, but for all that a strange, unnatural operation.

As zero hour approached we pulled out our protective glasses, so dark that they made even the bright Japanese sun look dim; but nothing happened. We circled, circled, circled. Properly speaking, we should have been in loose formation, but we had broken up because of bad weather on the way and the rendezvous had misfired; we were alone. Finally we gave it up and set course for the secondary target on the other side of the island—Nagasaki. Halfway across the Captain began to turn and said:

'Even a B29 doesn't fly for ever; we'll pack it up.' But after some hard words and some straight talking he changed his mind. Then, fifty miles away to starboard, the bomb went off. How pale by comparison Wilhelmshaven; how insignificant Bergerac. Yes, and with such utter devastation before our very eyes, how imperative to do something to see that it should never happen again.

If on the way out I had hardly been able to wait for my return to England, on the way back I could wait a thousand times less. In the files were signals that it would be eighteen months at least before the last of the overseas troops could expect a home posting, and that we must all exercise patience and restraint; but I could not help myself. I sent in applications, wrote personal notes, asked for interviews. Each day that passed was not just a day too long, but a year. At times ten years. Finally Air Ministry posted me to the Gulf of Mexico where I was to be the guest of U.S.A.A.F. and teach them low-level marking. But I would have nothing to do with it. I was told that the Americans were closing down on the exchange of technical information, and that since this was about the only thing that they wanted from us, the Chief of the Air Staff placed special importance on the posting; but still I would have nothing to do with it. Even if Winston Churchill himself—my hero of the dark days of 1940—had asked me personally I would still have turned it down. Anything, any price, just to get out of America back to England and on with the plan of world peace born in the skies of Nagasaki. And so, as was inevitable in a free country, I had my way.

But I returned alone, all hope of compromise between Constance and myself abandoned for ever.

Before Clement Attlee, the Prime Minister, who called for an account of what had happened over Nagasaki, I confided the plan. The Romans had once held the world at peace, and the world had been the gainer. With a really determined effort, and with the help of our lead in the field of atomic energy, we, the Allies, could now do the same. We could impose peace—for the world's good—by sheer, unanswerable force. Wasn't this better than the extinction of civilization itself? Wasn't it no less than our duty to those who had laid down their lives?

Mr. Attlee looked slightly startled, but continued to suck at his pipe in silence. So I proceeded with the argument, warming up as I went. The crux of the matter was private enterprise. It was private enterprise that had supplied the Armed Forces with the arms they needed and when they needed them; it was private enterprise alone that could now supply the drive necessary to win the coming armament race. In view of the urgency of the situation would he not continue the state of emergency? Would he not continue to mobilize the whole potential of the nation? In particular would he not authorize a privately run company for research into the development of atomic energy as a means of propulsion into space?

No, he would not. Definitely not. At the same time he was curious to know whether I had a concrete and constructive proposal to make? Because if so, let him have the outlines of it and he would consider whether or not it was worth while passing on to the experts.

This was asking a lot, for no one takes kindly to handing his favourite brainchild over to another, even though that other be the Prime Minister himself. However, there being no alternative, I did as I was told. The race, I said, would be won or lost not by the number or size of the atom bombs that a nation held but by the efficacy of the means of delivering them and the immunity of her stockpiles from destruction. The solution was to stop thinking in terms of conventional air-craft and rockets, in fact to stop thinking in terms of the earth at all, and to launch out into space. Yes, space—Mr. Attlee gave the impression of not having quite heard correctly.

What wonderful dreams the mere mention of the word conjured up! In space there was no atmospheric drag to contend with, even gravity itself became an asset. One could fly at the speed of light, cover unheard-of distances, or even, if one wished to, remain static for the rest of eternity. But to come down to Mother Earth—if the metaphor might be excused—the point was that in space one could suspend a satellite, or rather a whole series of satellites. Just think! They would stay up for ever; they would never need refuelling; they would just go round and round, like a kind of baby moon; and in them could be dozens and dozens of atom bombs waiting for the first blip of a wireless signal to come down on any target anywhere in the world. Wouldn't that put the fear of God into anyone who might be harbouring thoughts of war or aggression? Wasn't that a really practical way of making quite certain that we did at last have peace?

Mr. Attlee took his pipe out of his mouth, settled down a shade deeper into his chair, and steered the conversation on to generalities. The interview was over.

Shortly afterwards I was summoned to Air Ministry for

my final Medical Board and told that I was suffering from psycho-neurosis. A year's complete rest, they said, was the only hope. Such a helpful suggestion. Mother and Father begged me to take their advice, and offered me a year's holiday at home or anywhere in the world that I liked to mention, or a combination of both. But I turned it all down. I was in a mood to turn anything down, no matter where it came from or where it led to, other, of course, than the moon. For the moon lay in space, and in space I saw the key to peace, and peace now occupied the greater part of my thoughts. Yet not entirely all, for the *Sunday Graphic* had given me a contract for a fortnightly article at double the salary I had ever earned before. A new life was dawning.

With the end of war, society had come back to London. The Mayfair bar, for the best part of five years emptied of its customary beauty and glamour, had regained some of its lost ground. The Vanity Fair, latterly struggling to keep pace with its clientele's demand for American cigarettes, bottles of whisky, and other under-the-counter items, could now face its daily mounting membership with confidence and assurance. The night-clubs, which inch by inch had been yielding before the early-morning shortage of taxis, were now returning to their pre-war glory. For proprietor and client alike there was leeway to be made, lost opportunities to be snatched before they were gone again. For myself in particular there was the life of the Air Force to be replaced, there were doubts and frustrations to be drowned. At every turn the present was calling. Make the most of me while I am still here. Make the most of what is offered you and be thankful. Yes, be thankful.

By the end of the year I had taken a three-storeyed house in Kensington Gardens, engaged a cook and a butler—and, of course, a char, because it wouldn't have been quite the thing to ask either of the former to do the cleaning and scrubbing—and life had settled down into its routine. Get woken up at eight with tea; struggle out of bed at nineish, tea untouched;

partake of breakfast when strong enough to do so; discuss the domestic arrangements with the staff, and order lunch and dinner; start on a little correspondence and consider when to get down to the next *Sunday Graphic* article; drive down in the Bentley (acquired on a banker's overdraft guaranteed by Father) to the Mayfair—or possibly the Antelope—to take stock of the situation and settle a plan of campaign for the day. Decide at the last minute to stay on; ring up and cancel lunch. After a frustrating visit to the City in search of financial backing, return to the Mayfair for a breather, extend the duration of the visit on the off-chance of a useful contact, ring up and cancel dinner. Gravitate to one or other of the night-clubs, sit the session out; garage the Bentley and walk up Church Street approximately at milk-delivery time, think up a suitable apology to the staff, and decide to get down to things in earnest after breakfast. Occasionally, but only very occasionally, stay in for tea or supper and read a book on religion.

As a boy I had gone to church on Sunday, but not too regularly, and then only because I had to. At school itself I had survived my quota of Divinity lessons, and had even sat exams on Scripture without being failed. Once I had gone so far as to enrol in a Bible Reading Fellowship and had kept it up until the end of term. But with my departure from school— a term earlier than normal—what little I had managed to learn had vanished into oblivion, leaving a hazy mental picture of one or two isolated scenes, the most haunting of which was that of a lady hurrying through the night on a donkey with something clutched in her arms. Now gradually, as I read, the details began to fill themselves in, the picture to come to life. How different it all seemed—no longer a series of instructions to have preached at one; no longer a subject only for clergymen and other similarly minded people, and to be mooted in hushed and pious tones, but the story of a person. Yes, a person. One who though a God, the creator of all things visible and invisible, yet was interested in man's affairs, and who actually became man, out of love for man, and though rejected and condemned to death by those He had come to save had yet loved them unto the end.

But to give one's allegiance to a Person whose power was unlimited and whose judgement faultless, who had created heaven and earth and all that lay between, and yet who had walked this earth as we walk it, was one thing. To plunge into the clutches of an institution as impersonal and far removed from reality as the Church was quite another. For who could honestly maintain that the Church and its clergy were realistic, that they knew how to march with the times, that they faced up to the facts of life and death as if they knew what they were doing and had authority for what they were saying? Respectable men, kind men, understanding men, yes. But seldom men of action, seldom men who spoke as one would expect from the ambassadors of an Almighty and all-powerful God.

Then the mood would disappear, to give way once more to the Mayfair round. Only now a new element crept in, a more human one. If the pursuit of contacts brought little in the way of material help or of concrete proposals, it uncovered much in the way of restlessness and dissatisfaction; for beneath the outward signs of peace and victory lay cloaked many an inner conflict, with hope and uncertainty struggling one against the other. Hope because of the return of so many prisoners of war; hope because of the end of so much suffering, of so many separations, of such universal dread at seeing the telegraph boy cycling up the drive; hope because of the return of cigarettes and whisky, and of a bit of life and beauty to London; hope because of the advances that the war had brought in science, and of the promises that they offered. But also uncertainty. Uncertainty of the unknown, of having to find one's feet in a world where those who had not been called upon to fight were now in a safe and predominant position, uncertainty because of the changes that were coming over the spirit and outlook of the nation, of the almost overnight disappearance of the unity and determination which had held us together in the one boat and pulled us through the storms and gales; uncertainty that having gone to war in fufilment of an undertaking, and the promise being still unredeemed, we had any right to the spoils and claims of victory.

Under the strain of this inner conflict, values and standards began to change; space-ships and atomic energy, once so irresistible, faded from the limelight and in their place schemes and plans followed one another in a motley succession. Some were just fanciful and absurd, such as going out to fight in China, or forming a special duties team of volunteers to tackle the South Pole or the North Pole or any other inaccessible objective that scientists, or anyone else, might wish to explore. Others were more modest and practical—such as growing mushrooms in the disused tunnels of the Underground, or organizing a lecture tour on the subject of the threat of atomic war. But none, however grandiose or ambitious, however popular and well supported, seemed to satisfy; for in each there seemed to be something missing. But what?

How often I asked that question. How feverishly I searched, looking for it now in the City, now in the nightclubs, now when racing the Bentley through the country to let off steam, now when collecting material for the fortnightly article. But never apparently coming any closer, never achieving peace of mind.

Then one day I took my courage in both hands and called on the then Vicar of one of Hampstead's most famous parishes. Here at least I would come face to face with reality, even if at the cost of a certain amount of hardship and renunciation. But how little was I prepared for the answer I was to receive! 'I would like,' I said, 'to start at the beginning.' 'And what is the beginning?' he answered with a smile. 'That Christ is God, I presume.'

'Oh, so you start from the premise that Christ is God. Yes, of course it is true. But then so are we all. So are we all. You see, God is in all of us, all of us are in God. We all have a share of the Divinity. Christ merely had a greater share. He wasn't *actually* God; no one can be that. He was the son of God, just as we all are. There's a difference between that and saying that He is God, isn't there?'

Indeed there is.

4

EVENTUALLY, being fed up with the general moaning and groaning about conditions in Civvy Street, and confused by the widely different opinions of the clergy on the subject of religion, I gave vent to my feelings in the fortnightly *Sunday Graphic* article. Why, I asked, sit down and complain? Why not get up and act? If there really is disunity and self-seeking, why not counter it by unity and self-sacrifice? Why not take over a disused aerodrome and on it found a community of ex-Servicemen and women in which the strong would support the weak, the skilled the unskilled, the rich the poor, until all could stand on their own feet; in which, above all, the unity of purpose that had pulled us all through the war would prevail once more?

The response exceeded everyone's expectations. Letters of support and enlistment poured in by the hundred, and voluntary helpers by the dozen. The *Sunday Graphic*, for the first time genuinely pleased with the article, placed their printing press and secretarial department at our disposal. And Robinson the butler, partly out of sympathy for the fact that I had gone down with an attack of mumps, ran a non-stop bar and buffet service for the benefit of those who called to offer their services. Within less than three weeks we were able to summon a public meeting which was crowded to overflowing and presided over by one of Oxford's most learned Dons, Lionel Curtis, and which actually succeeded in coming to a few fundamental decisions. We would found a community which was to support itself by carrying on farming and other productive activities. Those who had a trade would be given priority and would set up and run their own businesses, handing in their profits to a central pool; they would undertake to teach those without a trade as soon as possible. Families, as well as single men and women, would be eligible for entry, and the management of the community would be entrusted to a representative committee. Everybody would receive their board and lodging and weekly pocket-money at the committee's discretion, but money would be the least consideration, and members would be expected to join in a spirit of service and altruism.

To handle the preliminary correspondence and requests for information, a small headquarters would be established somewhere in London and volunteers were called for to man it. Efforts would be made to find a site for the community, preferably a large estate with a farm, and a second meeting would be convened as soon as there was something definite to report. The question of money was raised, but it was felt that this was only of secondary importance and that the finances would be forthcoming without too much difficulty. By the time the meeting closed a long list of applications for the colony was received, and sundry gifts totalling over a hundred pounds were collected for the initial expenses of the office. Lionel Curtis wound up the proceedings by saying that a tiny flame had been lit which would spread all over the world.

In the absence of anything better and cheaper, we took over a dilapidated cellar under a friendly florist's, which had been written off as beyond repair and useless; and there began to pass before the astonished flower-girls' eyes a remarkable cavalcade of callers, some carrying pieces of building material, some dispatch cases, some just a hat, some nothing at all, but all hurrying and preoccupied as if intent on some urgent business. Amongst them, one morning, came a heavily built man in the uniform of a French-Canadian Major. He marched down the stairs in military fashion, circumnavigated a collection of packing-cases, junk furniture and odd-sized boards with which it was hoped to mend the floor, and bellowed out:

'Say, what's going on around here?'

Before any of us had time to answer him—or even collect our senses—the Major sat down at what passed as a desk and assumed control. The scheme, he announced, was a world-beater and a real one at that. Speaking for himself, he was going to throw up the Army and move in lock, stock, and barrel with his wife and family and all his possessions. He looked round the room, asked if we could do with some stationery and, without waiting for a Yes or a No, said that he would send some round. Then, having given us a brief, but powerful, pep talk, he marched up the stairs as firmly as he had marched down, turned round halfway up and said that henceforth he would like us to call him Robbie. Later that day four hefty Canadian soldiers staggered down the stairs with a six-foot-long packing-case full to the brim with paper, envelopes, files, pencils, and ink, all bearing an official seal but apparently for our unrestricted use. There was no doubt about it. The idea was catching on.

Our most pressing need, now that everyone was so anxious to make a start, was a property. But without money to pay for them, estates of several hundred acres with houses and farm buildings attached proved unusually hard to come by. So finally we settled on Gumley, a large and derelict house in the neighbourhood of Market Harborough which a trusting landlord offered us rent free, on condition that we kept it from falling down. There was no land other than a small circle of grass in front and a steep slope at the back running down to the lake, but what did that matter with acres and acres of fields as far as the eye could see, the owners of which would fall over backwards to give once they saw what we were aiming to do? With the signs of spring around us and the crocuses blooming in Green Park, the second and crucial meeting was held. So great was everyone's enthusiasm, enflamed by offers of support and goodwill messages from as far afield as Holland and Canada, that hardly a thought was given to the problem of how the colony would exist. The offer of Gumley was accepted, an advance party of eleven nominated, and the title V.I.P. chosen—Vade in Pace (Go in Peace). From the platform we announced that peace and understanding among men was our ultimate goal, and summoning up my courage I concluded the proceedings by saying that the foundation upon which we intended to build, and without which we couldn't hope to succeed, was the second Christian Commandment—Thou Shalt Love Thy Neighbour as Thyself. Someone objected that this was putting the cart before the horse; that the second Commandment was meaningless without the first.

Perhaps so. But it had cost enough to get as far as that, and the rest would have to be left to follow later.

For the three days immediately preceding the move to Gumley, Bedford Gardens was turned into an advanced field Headquarters-cum-despatch centre, much to the joy and relief of Robinson, the butler, and his staff. No doubt for size and efficiency it wouldn't have held its own against Hamilton Field, San Francisco, but for urgency and speed of movement it undoubtedly would. From early morning till late at night the door opened on a steady stream of callers, some of whom came with but a hurried message and left without setting foot inside the house, some for the better part of the day, others for the night as well. The bedrooms were converted into emergency dormitories, the drawing-room into a multiple office with two typewriters working non-stop, and the pantry into a ration and equipment store, into which (and out of which) rolled a remarkable variety of goods.

At intervals throughout the seventy-two hours there appeared, disappeared, and reappeared a five-ton brand new ex-Army lorry which we had bought on the grounds that it was one of the best buys in London, and which had absorbed the greater part of our hard-earned money. Robinson, now no longer butler, but one of the key figures in a special duties unit, acted as confidential liaison officer between the various groups of volunteers, at one moment coming to tip me off as to the likely merits of such and such a prospective member, at another giving a discreet look or cough by way of disapproval. Of all those present, he ventured to suggest—not meaning any disrespect, of course—the most enterprising and the best suited for any special operation was a certain wild-eyed Scot, nicknamed Jock, whose shock of black, uncombed hair had the extraordinary knack of hanging half over his forehead without in the least looking untidy.

On the final evening just as we had finished the movement order and settled which stores and equipment would be carried by whom, and how the rendezvous with those travelling from the North and the Midlands would be kept, there came a telephone call from the Gumley Estate Office to say that it was very much regretted but we would not after all be able to take possession of Gumley, anyway, not for several weeks. The Hall, as had been amply explained at the time, was full of the owner's furniture—his ancestral furniture, not just ordinary furniture—and it had been agreed that occupation would be dependent on the furniture being moved into safe storage. Well, things being what they were and petrol being still rationed, no contractor had been found to take it on. Even if one were found to make a start tomorrow, it would be three weeks at least before the Hall was empty, for there were stacks and stacks of furniture, and some of it, especially the china and glass, would have to be packed with great care by experts, and such experts were almost impossible to come by. And after all, it was only five weeks since the question of taking the Hall had first been discussed, and in the usual course of business it would be six months or more before one even thought of taking possession. So the Estate could hardly be blamed for not having managed to rush everything through so quickly. Not that the agent himself wasn't entirely in sympathy with our excellent cause, and indeed would like nothing better than to see us installed with the utmost despatch and the least inconvenience, but one had to face up to facts; and the plain fact was that the house was full of several thousand pounds' worth of furniture with not a single room cleared and empty. Facts were facts, weren't they?

Yes, indeed, facts are facts. But facts seldom come except in pairs, and the second fact in this case was that it was now ten-thirty at night, and the advance party had received their marching orders; some of them were God knows where—in the Midlands, in the distant North, probably for all one knew, already on their way; the files had all been packed into the lorry, and the lorry had left Bedford Gardens an hour or more ago. Were we to alert the police? To call in the B.B.C.? To have men stationed on the railways? Wouldn't it be easier to throw open the stables and for the party to make the best of it there until the furniture was moved out? Perhaps our presence in the vicinity would even be an actual asset to the Estate, for we could undoubtedly bring a bit of pressure to bear on the contractor.

There was silence from the other end of the wire.

But the following afternoon, outside the locked and bolted door of Gumley Hall, stood an agent who had every appearance of having bottled up his feelings far too long. As befitted his calling and upbringing, he retained his outward calm and dignity with perfect control, even while watching the hitherto abandoned and moss-covered drive filling up with a variety of equipment, vehicles, and human beings, each of which clamoured for some form of attention and disposal instructions. But when, heralded by the loud and solo strains of 'Loch Lomond' and the screeching of brakes, the lorry came to an abrupt halt at the entrance in such a way that it was difficult to tell whether the gatepost had been torn bodily from its moorings, or merely broken in half, the cork exploded. And can one wonder? But the cause of right and justice having been established and the call of duty vindicated, the past was forgiven and forgotten in favour of the requirements of the present moment. For these, even to the most disinterested observer, were hardly negligible. The stables and garages were opened up, rooms were allocated, stores unloaded, a temporary kitchen fitted out, and the Estate's official blessing imparted. Then having eaten our first meal, surprisingly good and varied considering the single primus on which it was cooked, we sat down to discuss our immediate programme.

The advance party had been chosen with a view to opening up the house and preparing the way for the others, not with a view to production; yet with less than £100 in the bank production was the main essential. By hook or by crook we would have to get into the house at the earliest opportunity and devise some means of earning money. Of all the suggestions for doing so—hundreds of them—kennels seemed the most practical, for the outhouses lent themselves ideally to the purpose, and one of the women due to arrive in the follow-up party was a trained kennel maid. So we sent her a wire asking her to come at once, and a scrubbing party was detailed to start work on the stables at dawn. In the meantime a works manager was appointed to investigate the possibility of providing workshops for the wood and metal workers, a secretary to deal with correspondence and callers, and a treasurer to preserve the already dwindling funds. Colonel Clarkson, the senior member of the party and the first to have put his name down at the inaugural meeting, was appointed O.C. the colony. And with that we went about our several tasks.

Then after three nights of harness-room accommodation, the Estate Office sent word to say that if we cared to provide the labour, the furniture could be moved into the south wing of the house and the wing barricaded off, after which we could move in to the rest. What jubilation!

But in the weeks that followed the Colony was to pass through many moods, of which jubilation was by no means the most frequent, for if the spirit was willing, the flesh was weak and faltering. With the increase in the Colony's membership, a working committee was set up, and a great deal of time was spent in arguing and discussing. In fact, we argued ourselves hoarse, and discussed ourselves dry. Ideas for industries and profit-making occupations—which at times kept the committee in session for the entire day—flowed in limitless profusion, and had it not been for the shortage of ready cash there is no doubt that there would have been put into effect a dozen or so hitherto undreamed-of schemes for making money. As it was, the different occupations were varied enough for a community a dozen times the size of ours. In addition to a forty-five-bedroomed house to be saved from collapse and brought back into a habitable condition, plumbing to install, electricity to connect, a broken gatepost to mend, there was a kennel, a woodworking shop, a small plastic manufacturing concern, an electricity repair service, a toyshop, a travelling twopence-a-week lending library and a resident artist willing to take on any kind of work. In response to our local enquiries for agricultural land, the lessee of the Estate kitchen garden offered to hand his lease over to us, including stock and of course, 'outgoings'. None of us liked to ask what 'outgoings' were, particularly in view of the confidential way in which they were mentioned, and if any of us thought that £500 was an excessive price to pay for them, our doubts were dispelled by the assurance that the offer had only been made for the good of the cause, and that from the moment we took the garden over we would earn an income of £40 a week. £40! Enough to keep the whole community housed, fed and electrified; so a special collection was made, the money scraped together, and the deal concluded. There was much beating of drums, much moving about at the double, and the news was spread abroad that the back of the financial bogey was already broken. Just to make doubly certain, and to cut the losses of selling through a middleman, a stall was obtained in Leicester market-place, and for want of volunteers Jock was delegated as salesman.

But this, as it later transpired, was a far from profitable move.

Amongst the twenty or fifty members who arrived in the two weeks following the opening of the front door of Gumley came an elderly man, hardly 5 ft. 7 in. high, with a rather wizened expression which could change with surprising speed into either pleasure or disapproval according to the circumstances of the moment. From the minute he arrived he looked and behaved as if he meant business; and his business, he said, was mice. Not, of course, that he had earned his living at mice, but he had taken them up on retiring and, let there be no mistake about it, they were a very paying business, very paying indeed.

For once in its short career the committee was not allowed to have a say at all. Dick Richards had not joined the Colony to argue with committees—good though they were—and not meaning any disrespect he had come to get on with a job of work, and his job was breeding mice and selling them to the hospitals as guinea-pigs. Millions and millions of mice was the target, and the whole lot to be sold off as guinea-pigs. He had brought his tools and the first three or four specimens to breed from; all he wanted was a lorry-load of timber with which to build the hutches, and a place to work where no one would bother him. A timber licence was obtained, the summer-house handed over for a mousery and for the next six weeks Dick locked himself away constructing tier upon tier of hutches. To the uninitiated eye, the hutches seemed remarkably big for mice, and when one day, unable to contain myself any longer, I asked for enlightenment, he replied that they weren't for mice at all but for rabbits. The place wasn't at all suitable for mice—far too much noise and too many children. Mice were very sensitive to their surroundings and liked a bit of peace and quiet, which evidently a lot of human beings did not. No, rabbits would be far more suitable. Equally profitable? Well, that depended upon how many one sold and what price they fetched; but by and large there wouldn't be a great profit in them, just a steady little trickle.

Ah, well, no doubt it was all for the best, and at least the rabbits served a useful purpose by distracting the children and keeping them out of the way; but every now and again they would escape and add to the general confusion.

But money-making and the problem of industries were not the only matters that exercised the wits and tact of Colonel Clarkson and his committee. Very early on came the problem of the allocation of rooms and of the domestic arrangements in general. Five per cent or more of the members were married, and not a few of these had children. In theory the housewives would entrust the domestic arrangements to the housekeeper, so as to leave as many of themselves as possible free to work in the industries. But in practice each had their own ideas on how the house should be run, on what type of diet should be provided for the children, what allowance should be made for those who preferred not to bring their children down to the common dining-room, how the cleaning should be portioned out, what time meals should be served, what accommodation they themselves should have and others should not have, and a dozen or so other issues of a similar kind. And life was by no means peaceful or easy.

In due course Robbie arrived in a Canadian Army lorry, complete with family, luggage and an assortment of packing-cases and furniture, a petrol engine, a band saw, a cat, and bursting with ideas. In Leicester, nine miles away, was a load of Y.M.C.A. furniture worth four or five thousand pounds, which he could obtain for seventeen hundred. Would we kindly let him have the money, and he'd nip off after dinner and clinch the deal? What, we didn't have it? Well, of all the ridiculous things to say; of course we didn't have it; no pioneer venture worth its salt had £1,700 lying in the bank. But was that any reason for turning the deal down? Could we not see that if done properly the purchase and re-sale could be handled simultaneously so that in all probability the only financial transaction to take place would be the transfer of £2,000 or so in our direction?

No, we could not see it. So he shook his head and said:

'Amazing! He throws away a fortune because he won't pledge himself to seventeen hundred pounds which he won't have to pay anyway.'

The next morning he walked into the office and asked where the crèche was.

'Crèche?' I answered, a little mystified.

'Yes, the nursery. Appoint one of the women as nurse in charge of the children, put all the children there during the day, and then send the wives to work.'

This time he was undoubtedly talking sense. We picked an ex-school teacher, a widow, initiated her into the scheme and asked her to take charge. Two days later the office was invaded by a deputation of mothers, one of whom was carrying a broken comb, another a dirty-looking towel. Both these interesting specimens were thrust under my nose, and I was asked whether if I had children I would like them to have their hair combed and their faces dried with these. Yes, THESE.

Robbie, however, was up to the occasion. He went to the wives, cap in hand, and told them that he had been working on a scheme for the manufacture of four-inch-diameter felt balls which could beat anything on the market and fetch in a net profit of a shilling each. With seven women working a fifty-hour week there should be a weekly output of 600 balls, that is to say £30 clear—the entire wage bill of the Colony. But it all depended upon finding five women who could sew, two who could use a pair of scissors, all seven of whom could work together as a team. Now where else was he going to find these except amongst the housewives? And how else were the housewives going to see him through but with the help of a crèche? The point needed no driving home. Within a matter of hours the crèche was reorganized, and the seven wives ready to start on the new industry. The moment was opportune enough, for one by one the existing industries had run into difficulties and setbacks. The stables were judged unsuitable for high-class kenneling—and nothing less than that, of

69

course, would do for V.I.P. The plastic manufacture department had failed to get a licence for raw material. The woodwork shop, whose foreman was the most skilled of all the Colony's craftsmen, could get nothing but unseasoned wood, so that the lampstands and ashtrays he turned out warped and cracked before they could be put on the market. The toyshop had succeeded in producing a number of most enticing samples, but no one could agree on their costing.

The produce from the garden seemed to sell all right, but somehow never brought in the returns it should have done—either, Jock told us, because it was a day too late or a day too early, or because there was a surfeit of lettuces on the market, or a deficiency of carrots on our part. Yet none of these setbacks served to daunt the office. From before breakfast until well past midnight its five desks and three typewriters were hard at work, with so much coming and going, so many letters being received, answered and filed, so many interviews, deliberations, drafting of reports, so many telephone calls from as far afield as Holland and even America, that it might well have been a United Nations in miniature. The books showed upwards of 1,000 actively interested prospective members, and twenty times that number passively interested. The growing public response, fostered and boosted by the fortnightly *Sunday Graphic* articles, made it obvious that Gumley was nothing more than a pilot scheme, that once the initial problems had been solved and the basic principles established, there was nothing to stop world-wide expansion. Already a search was being made for a second site—one where there would be sufficient land for agriculture on a large scale. The Colony was no longer looked upon as an end in itself, as a place where members came to stay for life, but as a training unit where teams for the overseas units could be equipped for some trade, trained in the special conditions of the place to which they were going, and then sent out with a ready-made plan.

Overseas expansion now became almost a household

expression; the horizon was widening, the vision growing in stature. Bedford Gardens was becoming less and less an oasis in the desert, a temporary refuge in which to draw breath and recreation, and more and more a *pied-à-terre* from which to invade the Commonwealth Offices and the City finance corporations. Even at that its period of occupation was growing increasingly shorter, its periods of disuse longer. A final push, one might almost think, and it would suffer the same fate as the Bentley—the auctioneer's hammer. And, indeed, the auctioneer's hammer, which had formerly lifted only to register yet another bid for some article of household furniture, now began to fall in support of Gumley's fast fading resources.

Under such circumstances as these, with the solvency of the Colony the last remaining obstacle in the way of a world-wide expansion, the felt balls came as a veritable gift from heaven—to the women an opportunity of saving the day where others had failed, to the men a challenge that could not be ignored. From behind the closed doors of the summer-house on the extreme north of the property to the last green-house on the south, there was a noticeable tightening of belts, a distinct air of determination and purpose that had not been there before. The lorry returned from Leicester with roll upon roll of first-quality felt and sack upon sack of discarded wool; a special set of tailor's scissors was ordered by telephone through Bedford Gardens; an emergency working party was detailed to clear and fill out a workshop; and work began in earnest under Robbie's watchful and eagle eye. A target indicator was designed and set up on the workshop wall where all who passed by could see it, and week by week the pointer began to rise: 110 the first week, 250 the second, 350 the third; £17 10s. a week. 'Just a question of a little tightening up in production drill,' said Robbie, 'and we're there.'

But the following morning Robbie burst into the Office, announced that he was leaving for a surprise visit to Canada, and was gone before anyone had grasped the significance of what he was saying. On his return, three weeks later, the pointer was just short of the 400 mark, waiting for the shop steward to give it the promised extra boost. The women had weathered the storm; they had good reason to be pleased with themselves, to expect a pat on the back. Robbie, however, had stumbled across a world-beating design for toys in Canada. With hardly a look at the pointer he announced that the balls were scrapped and that production would go over that very afternoon to the new project. It was the end of a beautiful dream. The women said but one word, 'Well!' and marched out, never to return. The toy-shop, for five happy weeks the scene of so much activity, and of so many admiring visitors, lapsed into disuse, with pieces of felt and handfuls of wool scattered over the floor for the children to stumble over and the mice to nibble.

5

BUT no sooner did one door close than another opened.
Early in September my aunt, Nancy Barstow, telephoned to say that she had heard that we were looking
for a property and wondered whether we would be interested
in buying Le Court, her family estate. The official price was
£35,000, but both she and her mother would far prefer that
it went to a cause such as ours, and if we wanted it they would
drop the price to £22,500.

What an offer! A twenty-five-bedroomed house, with
magnificent panelled halls, huge reception-rooms, 300 acres
of agricultural land, thirty cottages, outhouses galore, sweeping lawns, and unending flower beds. And into the bargain a
virtual gift of £12,500. What possibilities it opened up! What
old dreams it revived! Gone was the time of thinking things
over, of discussing in committee, of weighing one alternative
course of action against another, of worrying about the financing of home industries. Indeed, the call to action had sounded,
and all that was needed was a simple 'Yes'—or a simple
'No'.

Just a simple 'Yes' over the telephone to become the
owner of a £35,000 estate.

How simple it was.

Yes, but what headaches were to follow.

On the eve of the appointment for exchanging contracts
and paying the 10 per cent deposit, I found myself installed
in my Aunt Edith's Knightsbridge flat signing letters of appeal.

Signing, signing, signing. It was all I seemed to have done for a whole week. But everything else had failed, and what could one do? The money from the *Sunday Graphic* had all gone into the kitty. The Bentley had been sold—and practically everything else too. We had tried the City. We had pushed out circulars to the general public. We had tackled the Press. But all to no avail. Thinking that we were perhaps becoming too materialistic we had approached our Bishop and asked if he would be good enough to serve as a member of the Governing Body, but he had politely declined without offering a solution to our problem. This had been the last straw, and we had answered in some heat. The Church, we pointed out, had been steadily losing ground over the years; it was divided amongst itself; it could not agree even on its fundamental teaching; it had lost contact with the people; its influence on world affairs was steadily diminishing. Yet when the laity came forward of their own free will, and in good faith, to ask for help and co-operation, what was the answer? Sorry, too busy. Had we waited before answering, we would probably have written in a different vein, but things were getting on top of us.

So it happened that prayer gradually stood out as the only remaining hope, though admittedly a slender one, for prayer did not come naturally; and ask as one might, no one seemed able or willing to explain how to go about it—except perhaps Edith, who had her own definite views.

'Work, my boy,' she said, 'work, not prayer. Prayer may be all right in its proper place, but not when it's a matter of money. For money you've got to work. You've got to become a businessman—act and think like one. And that somehow I can't see you doing. It's a pity you won't listen to your old aunt. If only you did, you'd give up all these high and mighty ideas of yours and get down to earning an honest living, as the rest of us have to.'

The advice, no doubt, was good, and for a short space of time I felt like taking it as being an easy solution to so many problems. But on reflection, no. Far better to fight it out and keep on signing appeals.

Then in walked Father. It was a surprise to see him, for it was past five o'clock, and on his rare visits to London he invariably left early enough to get back to Mother in time for supper. He enquired how things were going, looked at the pile of appeals and then said:

'Lad, I've brought you a cheque for £2,250. I thought it might help.'

What could one answer? What words could one find worthy of the occasion? None.

Then, to cap it all, a friend in the City, Kirkpatrick, negotiated a mortgage for the rest of the purchase money and Nancy gave us an interest free loan of £8,000 to pay for the fittings, machinery and outgoings. We were home at last.

But for all its prospects, its rolling fields of farmland, its beautiful grounds, and fertile kitchen gardens, Le Court was not to prove the haven of our expectations. To some, its panelled halls and sculptured ceilings, its terraced lawns and shapely yew hedges spoke of a standard of living that they had never known, and in which they would never feel properly at home. To others, whom the luck of the draw had given an empty cottage, or a self-contained flat, the time had come for a period of security and family life, when the losses and stresses of the past six months could be recouped, the future made fast. To yet others, the estate, with its stables and cowsheds, its barns and outhouses, its greenhouses and well-appointed offices, offered endless opportunities of development and productivity which the management was throwing away for want of knowledge and capital; there was need for reform of policy, for more modern ways of thought, above all for competent leadership. Alone Robbie was completely in his element, and for a while his enthusiasm carried the community through the strain and exertion of the move. On a preliminary survey of the estate, a few weeks earlier, he had taken one short look over the forty-five acres of wooded parkland sweeping down from the top of the drive and had told Nancy, when she had come to have a last look at her beloved garden and estate, that we would build a scenic railway.

'Say, Mrs. Barstow, you would have thought this had been planned for nothing else from the beginning of time. Can't you see?' he had expatiated, sweeping his arm in a majestic arc, up and down, in and out of the undulations and the hollows:

'How it all fits in so perfectly? Why, we'd hardly have to construct a single foot of scaffolding. It's all there just crying out to be used. Can't you picture the crowds coming out from Portsmouth—the bus loads? And down by the gate we'll have a café. Can't you picture it?'

Aunt Nancy, as it happened, could not, but she was far too well brought up to say so, and she reserved her comments until next I saw her, when she enquired whether I was quite sure of what I was doing.

Yes, of course I was; what a peculiar question to ask. But Robbie's vision of a vast scenic railway, second only to Atlantic City, was not destined to last long. For on turning round from the top of the drive his eye was caught by the timber. And what else could timber spell to a Canadian but money? In this case not just ordinary money, but big money. Really big money.

'Skipper,' he said, bursting into the office at Gumley, 'we're in the dough.'

Even allowing for past experience, it was a welcome statement just at that particular moment.

'Do you realize what you've done? You've bought a £35,000 estate for £22,500 of which you haven't had to lay out a single brass farthing. The estate has got £20,000 of timber ready to be converted into cash for the asking. Suppose you merely take half of it—just so as not to be extravagant— that makes a free gift of £10,000 to be added to the free gift of the entire estate, which amounts to saying that you've pulled off a deal of £45,000 sheer profit. Can you beat it?'

For the first time since the early hours of June 7th, the office typewriters came to a simultaneous halt, and six pairs of gazing eyes were focused on Robbie.

'But it wouldn't be quite the thing to denude the estate of all the oak trees, would it?' I asked. 'I don't think my aunt would quite see eye to eye with me over that, especially as she belongs to the Society for the Preservation of Rural Hampshire.'

'Ah, I was waiting for that one. Evidently you don't know that logging was the first business I ever learnt. Well, we've been over the estate with a toothcomb. Before we marked a single tree for felling we checked that it was in line with at least one other. When two objects of equal size are in line with another, the second one is out of sight, isn't it? That means you don't miss it if it disappears.' And to emphasize the point he sighted along his arm as if it were a gun-barrel.

'In line, Skipper. Do you get me?'

To be perfectly frank, I did. I was much impressed. And by the time it had dawned on us all that lining up two trees depends on where you happen to be standing, and that the whole thing was sheer eyewash, it was too late. The contract had been drawn up and signed—for a fraction of the profit we had expected. Our morale had suffered a fatal defeat.

And so steadily and inevitably things went from bad to worse. So critical did the situation become that we were forced to cease financing the industries and to throw the responsibility on individual members—those, that is, who wanted to do so. The rest were offered work on the farm. It was a far from popular move. How, it was asked, could anyone be expected to run a business on his own and make it pay? How could a man both work and organize? How could he build up a clientele in a completely new district and find the time to go round marketing his own produce? And what if something should go wrong and the invested money were lost? Yes, things look different when it is one's own money at stake. But whatever the pros and cons, the rights and wrongs, it was necessity, not personal points of view, that governed the moment, and willy-nilly the policy was enforced.

Then came an unexpected offer of help from Kirkpatrick, the financier who had arranged our mortgage. V.I.P., he declared, was basically sound and merely needed a certain amount of reorganization and reorientation. The one mistake had been in giving priority to the industries, when in fact we should have concentrated on the land and built the farm into a specialist concern, capable of competing on the open market. Once we succeeded in doing this, the industries could be grafted on one by one and made to pay, and then there would be nothing to stop our growth and expansion. As a first step we should appoint a first-class professional bailiff, and pay him a normal commercial wage; the money would more than earn its way. Then we should decide as quickly as possible on one principal line of produce and set about finding the necessary capital. If we were interested in pursuing the matter further, he was more than willing to advertise for a bailiff, sift and interview the applicants, help us work out a concrete plan of action, and once it had been drawn up negotiate a capital loan. Once the City could see that we were organized on a businesslike footing he was sure that financial support would not be lacking.

Coming from the hard-headed, practical City, this was comforting news indeed, and the offer was welcomed with open arms. A general meeting was summoned, and Kirkpatrick himself came down to address it. So sure was he of the facts, and so obviously logical in his arguments, that when the scheme was put to the vote it was unanimously accepted, and when volunteers to work on the land were called for there was hardly a hand that did not lift. Nor hardly a heart that did not soar.

Meanwhile, encouraged by the *Sunday Graphic*, and urged on by the vision of a world-wide organization, I had bought a Mosquito—for a song, and on credit—and now set off in it for the Continent. First to Holland, where Prince

Bernhardt had a house to offer us and where a group of Dutch-men were preparing to send the first two members (of many to follow) to join Le Court; then on tour of the R.A.F. Occupa-tional Units; and finally to Berlin by invitation of the Deputy Commissioner. On the final stage of the journey we ran into trouble. The weather had been fine and clear at take-off, and we had paid little attention to navigation, other than visual map-reading, but from Hanover onwards it worsened, finally degenerating into thick haze. The compass, as it happened, was partially unserviceable and accurate only within eight degrees; we had no wireless, and our maps were old wartime ones which showed neither the aerodromes in current use nor the zones of occupation. To make matters worse, it was winter and night was falling.

But the skies of Germany had not lost their watchful providence, and in due course a control tower shot under the port wing. It was R.A.F. Gatow. But no sooner seen than it was gone, for on altering course to enter the circuit everything was lost in the haze of the setting sun. A mile or two to the north was a Dakota, evidently losing height on the final leg of its approach. Our only hope was to use him as a guide by catching him up, lining up on his tail and then forcing him out of the way. And this we did. Harry Parker, the flight engineer/acting navigator, remarked that the crew looked startled as we passed them; 'Shook 'em up, Skip,' was his actual expression, but for us it was now or never, whilst for them, equipped with radio and ILS, another circuit or two would do no real harm. At 100 feet we still could not see the ground, but passed over a beacon and decided to keep on descending. At thirty feet the first two lights of the runway came into view, but intercepting our approach at an angle of 25°, and we saw the flarepath party racing for safety like madmen. A steep turn to port, flaps fully down, and the wheels were rolling to a stop between two winking and friendly rows of lights. By old-time standards it was not a particularly difficult operation, but two years at a desk had

had its effect. And truth to tell the strain was beginning to tell. I suddenly felt old, and perhaps a little jaded.

The following morning I stayed in bed. After all, there were no appointments, no letters to answer, no meetings to address. The house was overflowing with every conceivable —and inconceivable—luxury, with butlers and servants uncountable, with marble baths and shower rooms, policemen patrolling the gardens, menus from which to choose what one would, a supply of drink that would have made even the Vanity Fair sit up, invitations to accept or refuse, masseuses and manicurists on call, a thousand and one selections of things new, things old, of things undreamed of. So why, with all this, get up for breakfast, or even after breakfast? Why not rather stay in bed and take it easy, when one could meditate on the hard, crystal hoar frost on the fir trees surrounding the lawn and listen to the distant sound of men at work building extra quarters for yet further guests, when one could ring the bell to enjoin silence or to have the curtains pulled, when one could sleep or not sleep, according as one would.

At midday the doctor called round (just as a matter of routine, of course) and said:

'Stay where you are, and build yourself up. A good healthy diet, a good book, cheerful company, and nothing else.'

'Nothing else? You mean literally?'

'Ha, hum. I see what you mean; yes, you can take a little alcohol. I meant, don't take things too seriously!'

At lunchtime my Australian host came in to see how everything was going. He was a brusque sort of man, with his countrymen's flair for being forthright without giving offence. He threw a book down on the bed and said:

'There. Read that and let's see what you think of it.' It was *The Robe*. Then he left me to my own devices. Everything was quiet; latterly there had been little time for meditation. I read the book from cover to cover, quietly, thoughtfully. In parts I found it good, at times even very good, but as a whole it was disappointing and frustrating, for it was nine-tenths fiction, the product of a man's imagination, and it was not fiction, however good or to the point it might be, that I had come to seek. If religion was just a matter of living a better life, of pious thoughts and uplifting reflections, then by all means let fiction have its place, let each man be free to do as he chooses, to build up his own doctrine, his own standards, his own heavenly castles. But if religion be more than this; if its concern be with cold and stark reality, with the fundamental truths behind the whole of Creation, with the purpose of life, with its beginning, its end, and all that lies beyond; if its object be to enable man to become truly a man, to grow to his full stature, to become master of the created universe; if all this, and more still, be so, then let religion treat with truth as truth demands; let its doctrines be scientifically propounded and authoritatively imposed; above everything let it show that it is dealing with reality, as we in the Air Force dealt when it was a matter of mastering the laws of aeronautics, of soaring out of the sight of land, of penetrating mist and darkness, of reaching our journey's end. Let it be one thing or the other, either rock or sand, either reality or thesis, but never a mixture of the two, never just gravel.

My host seemed faintly amused by all this. One mustn't, he hinted, lose one's sense of proportion. One must remember to relax; to be one with the boys, at least just now and then; to make up for the days when there was no entertainment, none of the fleshpots, just work from early in the morning to late at night. And for this what season could be more suitable than Christmas; what city more appropriate than Berlin, the meeting-place of East and West, the haunt of generals and refugees, the playground of the Victor and Vanquished alike?

Then the round of celebrations opened. Burst would perhaps be a better word, for in Berlin, filled with the spoils and loot of four victorious armies, and surrounded by the utmost extremes of luxury and privation, there was a sense of tension, a surge of inner turmoil, looking for an outlet. Nor was that outlet difficult to find, whether one was the Supreme Commander driving in a bullet-proof limousine, heralded by the wailing of police sirens and flanked by Army outriders, or a simple airman riding in the back of a five-ton lorry. Whether one drove to a diplomatic reception or hitch-hiked to a N.A.A.F.I. dance, one could be sure to find something to suit one's taste—from the Caspian, caviar; from Scotland, whisky; from the Rhineland, wine; from Denmark, cheese; from France, dancing girls; from America, the stars of swing and rhythm; from all the world, something. Something to speed the fleeting moment. A veritable maelstrom of desire and temptation, of human necessity and the opportunities that inevitably accompany it.

And into this maelstrom how many were not swept? Some of intent and with their minds made up; some merely curious and probing, willing to be pulled this way or that according to circumstances, some with their eyes closed and in innocence.

But even a maelstrom may serve a merciful purpose, for there is no mistaking its nature, nor whither it is heading. It may pull and may attract, but nobody can doubt the final result; and such is not always so with the subtler currents that can lurk under more innocent-looking waters.

There was one at least that Berlin Christmastide for whom this was true, one who on feeling the return of the attraction (stronger by far for its long hibernation) knelt down suddenly and prayed:

'O my God, I desire, yet I desire not. I am weak, yet I long to be strong. Grant me Thy strength.'

And granted it was. But in spirit, rather than in body, for on my return to Le Court in mid-January I felt listless and tired; minor things which before would have passed by unnoticed became a source of irritation; the machine felt as if it were running down; I was content to leave others to get on with their jobs.

.   .   .   .   .

Spring of 1947 was a long time in coming, so long that there were some who wondered whether they would still be alive when it did. For winter of that year was one of the coldest on record. At times there were shrieking gales, when snowdrifts piled up to roof-top height, and in places even higher; at times there was a deathly still, when the very atmosphere felt as if it were solid. As to which of the two was the hardest to support, common opinion was unable to make up its mind; but in Le Court itself, even common opinion, like the water in the taps, had come to a halt—so arctic were conditions within the house. The coal merchant had long given up the unequal struggle of supplying the household on credit, and such fuel as remained was reserved for cooking. Robbie, who like everyone else was responsible for paying his own way, had claimed the fallen branches in the woods as his prerogative, and supplied us with logs at two shillings a sack. His small gang of three sawed and hacked, heaved and swore, at one stage almost broke out into sweat, in an effort to supply the demand. But the logs were green and wet, and the flames, having expended their last reserves of strength in combating the moisture, were left with barely a flicker of light to brighten the shadows. Shadows, too, there were in plenty, for the electric light was failing. The old engine, installed in the early 1900's and whose flywheel had necessitated the building of an outsize cabin to enclose it, was nearing the end of its days. So was the supply of paraffin, housed in an equally outsize underground tank, which had mercifully been handed over full to the brim. Hot water was unknown, except out of a kettle. The younger generation resorted to beards rather than face the rigours of the bathroom, the older generation to what was left of the whisky bottle. For myself, halfway between the younger and the older, I bought three of the thickest vests I could find and stuck to them inflexibly day and night.

Kirkpatrick, meanwhile, had not been idle. Short of contacting I.B.M. for their latest prototype electronic brain, he had brought the whole machinery of the business world into operation for the selection of a farm manager. He had advertised, issued circulars, sent acknowledgements, sifted, re-sifted, checked credentials, filed, interviewed, scratched his head, obtained advisory counsel, and made out a statistical return, whereupon the machine had disgorged a short list, an even shorter list, and finally candidate number one.

So a farm manager was appointed. In his train followed a business manager. And to keep an eye on things generally (a sort of Senior Administrative Officer, one might say) there came a retired army colonel, Pat Weddell, together with his wife, Wendy; he very much a stickler for law and order, she insisting that she would have nothing to do with administration or committees, but would scrub, or do the chores, or anything nobody else cared for.

Then in April winter gave way to spring. The sun shone, the fields sparkled, the birds laughed and sang; only the children looked slightly sorry because their toboggans would no longer run properly. There were other changes, too. The farm was going over to intensive cultivation, the greenhouses were being torn asunder to provide a more economical lay-out, hedges were being uprooted, machinery being ordered by the ton. From the City came a publicity firm to organize a national appeal for funds. They photographed, they collected statistics; they wrote a filing cabinet full of copy. The response, they said, would be enormous.

With this I fell ill and retired to bed. Pat stuck a barrier along the corridor leading to my room with a notice reading 'No business, no visitors'. The doctor ordered: 'A year off work completely. Preferably abroad'. Wendy, whose vivacity and love for doing the dirty jobs had thrived and multiplied on the cold and the difficulties of the past, took charge of me, and the joint managers charge of the Colony. All round my room, piled high in trunks and in packing-cases, were remnants of Bedford Gardens' past and forgotten glory. Through the window lay the rolling lawns, and the still immaculate hedges and flower beds, all of which, it was now being said, would have to be put to the plough in the interests of efficiency and economy. But this never; business world or no business world, never this.

The Vicar, on hearing I was ill, came to call. He advocated confession. Confession, he expounded, was the appointed means whereby we were absolved from our sins. To confess sincerely and to receive absolution was to start all over again, to begin again once more with a clean slate. It was consoling advice and in any case the Vicar was an understanding and helpful man. What else was there to be done but signify one's assent?

Then a day or two later a little booklet arrived in which were set out the rules of procedure, some homely advice, and points for self-examination. 'Have you been uncharitable in thought, word, or deed? Told lies? Been disobedient, angry, vain? Have you taken the name of God in vain? Sworn falsely? Or rashly? Or profaned the Sabbath Day?' What a mountain would have to be cleared before getting down as low as that—or should one perhaps say high? 'And having discovered the different sorts of sins of which you have been guilty, you should try to feel heartfelt sorrow for having committed them.'

But to feel sorrow under such circumstances is by no means easy, and when on walking through the woods to keep the appointment the spire of Greatham Church came in sight, it was all I could do to keep on walking, let alone be sorry, or humble, or even remember the things I was supposed to say. The Vicar, who was already waiting, received me with kindness and led me into the church. He locked the door behind him and we walked down the aisle—elongated, one had the impression, to a thousand miles. Then into the Sanctuary and across to a corner where a chair and a kneeler had already been set out. Not merely one, but two, I noticed, were showing signs of nervousness. I knelt down on the kneeler, took the pamphlet from my pocket and read out the introductory prayers, though whether it was the introductory or the concluding one I could not tell from the sense, only from the mark I had made in the margin. Had there been some reasonable means of escape I would gladly have taken it, but there was none. The Vicar was waiting for the confession. Halfway through it I broached the subject of Constance. Had I done wrong in separating? Ought we to make it up and return? And if not, where did we stand ourselves? Were we free to marry again, or not? He was not quite certain, for it all involved some deep theological principles. He would go and consult his Bishop and let me know. Deep theological principles! No wonder the untheological are liable to lose their way.

Then finally the confession was over. The Vicar cleared his throat and spoke a few words of consolation. Perhaps he also said a prayer or pronounced some absolution, but if he did it passed unnoticed. I stood up when he so motioned me, and we walked back the way we had come. Out in the sunlight, perhaps for want of anything more sensible to say, I asked how one could be sure that one had in fact received absolution. He gave me a piercing glance at this and said:

'But you don't doubt it, do you? If you doubt it you are undone. It's entirely a matter of faith; as you believe, so it will be done to you.'

'No, I don't doubt it. At least, I don't think I do. I'm just ignorant; I just don't know. But I do feel a little better, and that's something, isn't it?' Anyway, the tension was broken. Thank God, thank God.

Soon afterwards Wendy came bursting into the room like a runaway pony over the paddock fence at last:

'There's *the most* wonderful news,' she said. 'A monk is coming to see us. A real live monk. I've just this moment had the letter.' Then she sat down and looked at me:

'And, oh, Leonard dear, I've heard such absolutely wonderful things about him. Brother Hugh is his name, but he likes to be called Hugh, not Brother Hugh—you must be very careful not to forget that. He's associated with that astonishing man, Brother John, who eats practically nothing at all and

86

sleeps on a bathroom floor in Germany doing the most amazing work. Franciscan. And you mustn't—you *mustn't* breathe a word of this. Promise you won't? In fact, you mustn't even remember that I've said that, but I think, I think, that with just a little bit of persuasion he might come and help us. But you won't even remember that I've said that, will you, Leonard dear?'

'Oh, no, Wendy, of course I won't. How could I? The only thing is if I don't remember it, what about that persuasion you say we'll need?'

'Oh, I do wish you wouldn't always be so logical. You men are always the same, absolutely impossible.'

And there was Wendy flying out of the room again, to scrub or cook, or exercise Endless the Dachshund, or something of the sort.

Then Hugh himself arrived. He was short but verging on the stout side, and in spite of grey hair had a remarkably healthy-looking complexion. He walked into the room with measured steps, his head pressed down into his shoulders, as if immersed in thought or supporting some heavy burden, and advanced several feet before becoming aware that there was anyone in front of him at all. Then his face broke into a broad smile. His long black habit, which fitted tightly round his neck and stretched down to his feet, was held round the waist by a silk girdle, the tassel of which he kept patting and smoothing as he talked. And we talked a long time, helped by a bottle of port and a copious supply of cigarettes. But finally, when the request had been duly put to him, and after he had looked long and hard at the ceiling, he said that he would willingly come and join us.

So at long last the picture was complete. To a business-like and professional administration was now added our own private chaplain, an official representative of the Church of England. And what better representative of the Church could one have than a monk, living under a vow of poverty, desiring nothing for himself, wishing only to serve and give. Granted the household did not view the prospect quite in the light that I did, granted that when Hugh spurned the bed he was offered and said he would far prefer to sleep on a sofa or some out-of-the-way corner the Works Manager remarked 'Peculiar, very peculiar'; granted that when I explained how Hugh was inter-denominational and therefore the only man capable of minis-tering to us all, Paddy Thompson, ex-R.A.F. fitter from Ulster recently turned Catholic, screwed up his face as if he had just swallowed some indigestible object which would neither go down nor come up, nor melt nor leave him in peace. But in the end sincerity and self-sacrifice would win the day, and Hugh would become part of the family.

By early May arrangements had been made for me to spend my year away from work in the wilds of British Columbia with Bishop Embling, a long-standing family friend. And he, obviously, would take me in hand. He would give me the instruction I wanted so badly, but had never succeeded in getting. And while I was away Le Court would prosper and grow, the more surely because of the addition of Father, who had just come forward to say that he would accept responsi-bility for its affairs during my absence. The outlook was indeed rosy and bright. Too good to be true, one would almost think. But yet there it was.

Then finally a deputation from the Colony trooped in to announce that they had something of importance to deliver. I wondered what. Perhaps an ultimatum? Or a telegram with some bad news? But no, a six-week-old poodle puppy, the fluffiest and most mischievous ever to have been seen since the days of Simon. And just in case there should be difficulty in getting him through the Customs, his home-made portable kennel (much more like a house than a kennel) was painted in the boldest possible type with the letters V. I. P.

6

HAVE you by any chance ever had an attack of the creeples? Because if you have, you will be thirsting for an authentic account of its nature and symptoms. Whereas if you have not, you must be positively panting.

The word 'creeples' is not to be found in any textbook, dictionary, journal, or other weighty document of the medical profession; neither is it ever voiced on medical lips. The truth is that were the profession ever to join issue with the creeples, whether it were with a view to restricting their activity, or to establishing a foundation for research and investigation into their properties, or merely to extracting a fee from their victims, it would be inevitably worsted. Wherefore discretion has been judged the better part of valour. From this it follows that an attack of the creeples cannot be described in direct terms, but only in a roundabout and most circumspect manner. For example, it might happen that one was lying in bed contemplating the happy fact that never within the reach of memory had one been more happily placed, with so many hours of interrupted sleep ahead. One is in the actual process of falling off, enveloped in a beautiful haze, sinking, sinking, sinking. Suddenly, in the lower reaches of one's right calf there is a sudden twitch. Just the mildest, most innocent little twitch imaginable. But enough to scatter all thoughts of sleep, all happy contemplation of hours in bed to come. One kicks one's leg, massages one's calf, reads a page of a book, and lo! not a sign of the intruder. Ah! Blessed relief. Back under the bed-clothes once more. Everything peaceful and drowsy. The hours of sleep ahead extol their charm. One is on the actual point . . . another twitch. Still another. Get up, kick, massage. No means of catching the offender; he is gone. The awful truth strikes home that it is only on the verge of sleep that he exists at all. A single movement of muscle, a single positive thought, and he is not merely gone, he has ceased to be. How deal with an adversary such as that? How expect the medical profession to deal with an enemy that only exists in their absence, and whose only object is to expose their limitations?

But take the case of a man travelling to a strange land by one of the world's airlines. He has worn himself out in the process of selecting, from innumerable possibilities, the clothes and other paraphernalia he requires; he has miraculously managed to close his luggage and conceal its true weight; he has filled up countless forms, said his farewells, had his inoculations, and has remembered too late five articles of vital importance that he has forgotten. He has been informed that his plane is delayed, then frantically alerted, then de-alerted, then rushed out to the aerodrome like a madman, because it is now touch and go whether he will catch the plane at all. Once out at the airport he has been told that the plane has turned back to its departure point, and that there is an indefinite delay. Finally he is at his seat. It is midnight on the following day. All he can think of is sleep. But the thoughtful Company has showered him with literature describing the ineffable luxury of the means of travel he has so wisely chosen; and he is clearly expected to read it. At intervals, while he is settling himself back into his seat, he is asked whether there is anything he would like—a magazine, a cigarette, chewing gum, black coffee, a blanket? And as often as he shakes his head he is looked at reproachfully. Is there something wrong? Is he feeling ill—or perhaps not accustomed to air travel? Isn't there *anything* he would like? Yes, indeed there is; but before he can say what it is there is an interruption; a loud-speaker has come into operation; it announces (in dulcet, but no uncertain, terms) that there will be forms to fill in en route and precautions to be observed on arrival at the other end; it issues instructions to be followed in the unlikely (but not to be ignored) event of the aircraft shedding its wings and diving headlong into the sea; it offers practical advice on how to conduct oneself in the air; it is sure that the passengers would like to know the probable height of flight, the estimated time of arrival (in approximate terms), the wild guess the met. expert has made at the weather, the Captain's name, the co-pilot's address—or did he mean the air hostess's? And so it goes on. Overhead, along the centre of the ceiling, have been fixed a series of searchlights, so cunningly contrived that any one of them can shine directly into eight pairs of eyes at once, irrespective of how their owners may twist and wriggle and squirm, and these are in league with the Company's secret designs; they forbid so much as a mention of sleep.

Suddenly when all hope of rest has long been abandoned and it is practically time to prepare for disembarking, the searchlights are extinguished. There is every possibility of a whole hour of comparative darkness. From one's neighbour comes the faint sound of snoring. One settles back, closes one's eyes, determined to seize the opportunity. Sleep appears on the distant horizon. It approaches step by step, first from this quarter then from that, gradually gaining confidence as it comes. There is a sudden twitch. Sleep, which was oh! so close, retreats in confusion; peers from behind the curtain to discover the cause of alarm. There is another twitch; yet another. Sleep is frightened out of its wits; it races away, too petrified even to stop and look round; it is not even to be detected on the most distant horizon. The creeples have won the day. One wonders if one will ever survive the journey, and if one does whether irreparable harm will not have been done to one's state of health.

But the journey, as all journeys must, eventually comes to

an end. The train, which for twenty long hours has taken the place of a series of aircraft, has come to a halt at a small, busy station. In the distance are to be seen the shadowy outlines of mountains; but it is the immediate surroundings that are of greater interest. There are men wearing check-pattern shirts of highly coloured hues, others with tight-fitting blue canvas trousers, so tightly fitting as to give the impression that they have been in position, and thus grown up, ever since birth. The women were clearly not born, nor brought up, to idle away their time at the bar of the Vanity Fair, for they walk about on their business, hither and thither, as if they knew exactly what they were after, and brook no interference. All in all, there is an atmosphere of action, a tinge, one would almost say, of the pioneering days, when if we are to judge by what we are told, men *really* were men, and not at all as they are now. But the platform holds a great variety of dress and character and age; and towards the far end there is a tall, elderly man with a bronzed and ruddy complexion. He has a clergyman's collar round his neck, ecclesiastical gaiters on his legs and a Pectoral Cross on his breast. He is a Bishop. He starts forward on recognizing a once familiar face, and then stops for a moment, his chin protruding and his jaws working, as though chewing an anticipated but knotty problem. From the portion of the train towards which he was making his way is being unloaded an uncommonly weighty pile of luggage, not to mention a raincoat, a town coat, a country coat, a bear-skin coat, two hats, a gold-headed malacca cane, an umbrella. Ah! yes, and last of all a curious-shaped wooden box with the boldest imaginable lettering on it, and inside the smallest and most mischievous ball of fluff ever seen. The guard who supervised the unloading, and who is of no mean muscular proportions, examines the inside of the box and discovers to his astonishment that the straw is as dry and clean as the day, seventy-eight hours before, when it was put in. The same, however, cannot be said of the platform, which the ball of fluff has seized upon as if it were the oldest and longest-lost friend in the world. The Bishop, who has now arrived within earshot, surveys the scene with a practised eye, and without a word by way of introduction says:

'I don't think you are going to need an umbrella out HERE.'

There is a wealth of meaning in that simple word HERE; so much so that its recipient has a momentary spasm of fear and says to himself: 'My God, what have I done? Have I made a complete fool of myself?'

But it is not the time for mental spasms, nor for creeples. The Bishop, who is evidently a fighter by nature and used to action, has the air of one who has been expecting a troublesome time ahead and is steeling himself to meet it, for he will stand no indecision or abstractions. On the sixty-five-mile drive that follows there are greetings to exchange, matters of the immediate moment to resolve, memories of long-past, half-forgotten days to revive. There is also scenery of unparalleled grandeur to marvel at, towering mountains and bottomless ravines; gigantic trees and scuffling squirrels; a profusion of natural wonders to absorb the eye.

On reaching home there is a house to inspect, all built in wood too; introductions to be made; a steaming hot lunch to eat. Then, when a long overdue mention of rest and relaxation is made, the Bishop gives a kind of silent, yet startling snort. Never in his life, it appears, has he heard such absolute nonsense. No, never. He leads the way into the garden to explain the lay of the land; to inspect the outside of the church; to glance at the lake, visible in gaps between the trees and houses. The ball of fluff comes too, and before anyone quite knows what is happening finds himself being briskly walked into the middle distance. If mention is made of the need for taking it easy, after seven weeks of virtually being confined to bed, the pace is merely stepped up. The policy clearly doesn't pay, and has to be abandoned. In any case, there is a running commentary to listen to on the different facets of the rapidly changing countryside—the trees, the birds, the rock formations, the spot where a wild cat was last seen, the feats of the lumberjacks, the log cabin in which lived an entertaining man who had succeeded in constructing a hydro-electric power station little larger than a car but which nevertheless gave light to the whole village, and of how, if only we stepped it up a little faster, we would reach the tomb of a man whose epitaph read: 'Who lifted a 1,400 lb. weight and then died'.

Under circumstances such as these both creeples and mental spasms are fighting a losing battle. Sleep hovers around the corner and is seldom obliged to retreat in confusion. The days pass. Muscles harden. The ball of fluff grows up until he thinks nothing of going a full day's trek through the timber, or sitting hour after hour listening to the sound of axe and saw, and dodging the falling trees. He chases smells, bounds after birds and squirrels, and on one occasion goes so far as to run in the wake of a bear. One would say that he is gradually becoming absorbed into the intimacy of the forest itself, for the time comes when the birds take him for granted and settle within reach of his paw, and when the squirrels, having once grown tired of tick-tick-ticking away faster than the speed of sound, come down from the heights to keep him company. But neither he nor they, for all their intimacy, are able to fathom the full depth of the forest's secret, for their concern is with time, not with eternity. They gaze at the roaring torrent cascading down from the snow-capped mountains and think of ice-cold water to drink or to splash through, not of the millenniums of man that it has outlived, and will outlive still, nor of how they have planned and re-planned, conquered and been conquered, come and gone, while it has remained just as it is, just obediently falling. They leap through the virgin forest and conjure up dreams of food to eat and quarry to chase, but they do not picture earliest man, the great pioneer, who once set out alone and unaided on his gigantic task to subdue an untamed virgin earth, and in so doing to subdue himself. They penetrate to regions where there is no sign of human life, no sound save that of wind and water and the rustle of branches, where they are wholly in their natural element, but they do not feel the pervading silence enfolding them as if it were a mantle, shutting out the chilling wind of distraction and noise, and generating an inner warmth of soul and spirit. Indeed, how should they? Would they be more truly themselves if they did; or we more truly ourselves if we did not?

But if they cannot guess the secret of the forest's inner life, still less can they guess the secret that lies behind the swing of the axe and the rhythm of the saw, still less can they follow the strange sequel to an evening's casual reminiscence.

The Bishop had occasion, and to spare, for reminiscences. After four years on active service in the First World War he had gone to Central Africa as a missionary, from there to West Bengal, and from there again to North Korea as a Bishop of the Church of England. He had never been what the politicians would call a Party man, in the sense of saying what was expected of him rather than what he honestly believed, nor had he ever minced his words when he felt that there was something to be said. With his own Church he was not afraid to find fault when the occasion demanded; of other Churches he was more ready to speak well than ill. When a local paper ran an out-and-out attack on Roman Catholics, he was the first to defend them; and it was not unknown that he would uphold their fervour and 'loyalty to tradition' as an example to his own parishioners. When asked what the difference was between Catholics and Protestants, he answered, 'Transubstantiation,' but in such a way that not the boldest man would presume to ask what that meant, nor to question him any further. When requested to explain a point of doctrine or to discourse on the art of prayer, he tossed his head and answered: 'I'm not a potted-meat artist. Go and find out for yourself.'

Rather than teach he liked to reminisce, and if in the story there was a moral to be found, then so much the better—as, for example, in the incident of the Scripture exam in the Theology College. It was all many years ago, long before anyone else in the room had learnt to read or write, but none the less worth the telling for all that. The students had been set an essay on the Nativity, in which they had been allowed to concentrate on any one aspect that they liked. One of them had chosen the Virgin Birth, and though what he wrote was in the true Anglican tradition, he had quoted the words: 'Hail Mary, full of Grace, the Lord is with thee.' The examiner had scored this out in blue pencil and written in the margin 'Dangerously close to Roman Catholicism'. But the second examiner—for it is apparently a custom not to trust just one examiner in a theological college—had overscored the blue with red and written: 'Much more dangerously close to Luke i, 28.'

There had been a general burst of laughter round the fireside, and indeed there was no doubt about it that it did make a good joke, especially as told by the Bishop, with his chin protruding and his jaw working hard, as if to say: 'I'll teach any Professor who starts monkeying around with a lot of stupid nonsense.' But a joke whose point one hasn't quite seen can't be dismissed just like that. And this one is not easily seen by the uninitiated. A man is told to answer a question on the birth of Christ. He quotes from the relevant part of Scripture, but alters the normal reading 'Highly favoured' to 'Full of Grace'. Nothing very sinister in all that, yet it earns for him the dire accusation 'Dangerously near to Roman Catholicism'.

In what, might one ask, consists the danger? Not in quoting Scripture, surely, for that would be equivalent to saying that to quote Scripture is to league oneself with Roman Catholicism, and somehow that hardly seems to make sense. Then perhaps it is in misquoting it? But this hardly makes sense either, for according to the Authorized version the correct translation is either 'highly favoured' or 'much graced', and what difference is there between that and 'full of grace'? Then in what *does* the danger consist?

Ah, the Bishop suddenly lets it out in the course of another conversation. 'Hail Mary, full of grace' is the beginning of a Catholic invocation—whatever that might be; and the danger lies, not in what the student quoted, but what he left unquoted.

But this becomes an even greater mystery than ever, and for the very reason that the Bishop doesn't disclose how the invocation continues, nor what its significance is, nor even what danger there can be in coming close to Catholicism, there wells up a great desire to know. No use asking the Bishop, because one feels a fool asking questions that one ought to know and then being told that one must go and find out for oneself. No use looking in the Church library, for one does not know what to start looking for, neither is it likely that a thing of danger will be found in *there*. Still, look one must, for having got as far as this it is impossible to give up.

So the days continue to pass. The axe flies faster and truer. The saw works more evenly and regularly. The ball of fluff bounds further and further into the timber, higher and higher above the timber-line. Summer shows signs of passing its peak. Then when least expecting it, while idly (and curiously) turning over the pages of a prayer book in a bookseller's shop in the railhead town of Nelson, there suddenly leap out the words:

Hail Mary, full of grace,
the Lord is with thee;
Blessed art thou among women,
and blessed is the fruit of thy womb,
Jesus.
Holy Mary, Mother of God,
pray for us sinners now,
and at the hour of our death.
Amen.

Very curious, for except for the petition at the end—and who in their right mind could object to that?—every single word is a quotation from Scripture, indeed the greater part of it spoken by the Archangel Gabriel in his greeting to the

Virgin Mary. And if Scripture sees fit to record it, then can there be danger for us in repeating it? How could anyone do other than encourage the world to pray it? How dare the Church recommend the prayers composed by men in preference to that of an Archangel?

And if the truth of the argument be in doubt, then let those who will prove it for themselves. For the Hail Mary, once learnt, rises spontaneously and easily from the heart, wherever one may be and whatever one may be doing—in rhythm with the swing of the axe, in time to the marching of one's feet, in harmony with the sigh of the wind through the timber. And as the habit grows, whether in the silence of the mountains or to the crash of falling trees, there descends a great and hitherto unknown peace; not just from the external surroundings, as previously, but from within, in the depths of one's soul, falling like the dew, one knows not how nor from where, bringing life to what was arid, softening what was tense.

7

SHORTLY before Christmas a cable arrived from Hugh saying: 'V.I.P. in trouble. Return immediately'. And since Hugh was clearly to be trusted I jettisoned everything bar the bare essentials and caught the first available plane home, thanks to the financial help of the Bishop. Mother and Father had not been consulted about the cable, and strongly disapproved, for although it was certain that V.I.P.s was going on the rocks and that the new management was no more successful than the old, they felt that health should have been put first and some interim measure taken to tide over the remaining four months.

Then, as soon as the Christmas festivities, such as they were, had subsided, we held our general meeting to decide the future. The issue was really a foregone conclusion, for what was there left for us to try? We had tried private enterprise, we had tried the City, we had tried the land, we had tried my being out of the picture, and it had all failed. To add yet a further complication, a serious crack had developed in the foundations of the house, and there was the likelihood of a heavy expenditure to shore them up. We could revert to the private enterprise system—for those who wished, but no one did so wish. We could organize a completely new line of business, but no one had any suggestions as to what the new line could be. We could issue yet another 'backs to the wall cry', and work up a new burst of enthusiasm. But somehow it didn't seem the time and place. Instead we gave it up. V.I.P. was formally announced a failure.

The actual decision was taken on the friendliest of terms, with mutual expressions of gratitude and regret. But the process of dispersing the community and winding up its affairs was another story. The majority of members, particularly the married ones, had nowhere to go. In joining V.I.P. most of them had burned their boats and invested a good part of their capital in the move. Many of them felt they had been hard done by, and that the management was wholly to blame. Perhaps it was, but we had all done the best we could. Nearly £6,000 of public gifts had been sunk into the venture, and it had all gone. Leaving aside the purchase of the estate, a further £5,000 had been given in the forms of loans. We had all shared equally in the benefits of this, and no one but the management was being asked to repay the creditors. The original promise to refund the £50 membership subscription would be honoured, and all those who could clearly show that they had invested money in the industries with consequent benefit to the estate would be given some compensation. But beyond that, there was nothing to be done. A stone can only yield a certain amount of blood. In lieu of compensation for their lost prospects, there were some who asked for a portion of the estate, or the free lease of a cottage, or some of the fittings and furniture. But there were also others who renounced all claim to the money they had invested—in two cases amounting to a matter of over £1,000; and others again who wanted to stay on, free of remuneration, to help recoup the loss and settle the claims of those who were in despair.

How, amid such conflicting points of view, adjudicate between so many different claimants? How decide the future of the estate? Let alone a future career? Whom to turn to for advice and guidance? Pat Weddell, the eldest of the community, who was ready to stay or leave according as he was requested, was the obvious choice for the post of adviser; but he was out of his element when it came to settling claims from a non-existent fund, and asked to be allowed to stick to the routine correspondence and the garden—the latter of which was now in a sad state of neglect and abandon.

Hugh was the second choice, but he had not wholly won the confidence of the members, nor could one always see eye to eye with his practical judgements, and to make him co-adjudicator was likely to be an unpopular move. Still, the essential thing was to do justice, not to please the majority. Moreover, if the future was to be built on a secure foundation and the mistakes of the past rectified, the old and false values would have to be replaced by more spiritual ones; the promptings of an unenlightened nature would have to be subdued; one would have to submit one's judgement to that of an elder and better. And this could not be done without violence to one's instincts and one's old ways of thought. So for better or for worse I asked Hugh to be my guide.

To this invitation he responded neither too eagerly nor too indifferently. We should take it all very quietly, he said, with neither too much work nor too little, neither too few spiritual conversations nor too many. For instance, we would be well advised to spend Sunday morning neither in work nor in spiritual conversation, but relaxing in front of a good warm fire discussing some interesting topic or reading the paper. Every now and then we could make an excursion to London or elsewhere to call on people of interest, to discuss ideas, or just to get a change of environment. It would all play its part in putting things in their right proportion and in building up the great future for which Le Court was surely destined—but which one couldn't quite foresee. Not just at present.

Indeed one could not. One could neither foresee Le Court's future nor any future at all, nor even see the slightest semblance of daylight anywhere at all.

Gone was the atmosphere of the early happy days when blind alleys and obstacles were but so many opportunities to prove one's metal, when we were all one united team following the same trail, whether it was false or true. Instead there was a feeling of tension, an awakening to the fact that it was now *sauve qui peut*, each man to find his own way out as best he could. If he could. Even the house itself seemed to have joined in the conspiracy, and had assumed the proportions of a dark labyrinthine maze from which one imagined there was no hope of escape. The old electric light engine had shed its flywheel, under the very nose of a startled Paddy, and was fit for nothing but the scrap heap. Such lamps as could be found had insufficient candle-power to light the common rooms, and everyone was forced to the seclusion of his own apartment, where behind closed doors he discussed and planned his own particular means of escape. The corridors and halls, of which there were plenty, were plunged in gloom, broken by an occasional shadowy figure hurrying along with a torch or candle. The huge central staircase, encased in a double tier of polished granite pillars, took on, under the flicker of a single faltering lamp, so sombre and menacing an appearance that only by gritting one's teeth and clenching one's fist would one succeed in braving it on one's own after dark.

As often as opportunity offered, I would seize the gold-headed Malacca walking-stick—one of the bare essentials salvaged from British Columbia—and take to the roads and lanes of Hampshire in search of a way of escape. But I found none. Through my head flowed a flood of ideas and plans, tumbling one over the other in a bid to gain a lead, but there were too many currents from opposing directions, too many twists and turns in the river bed, too many backwaters and channels without outlet, ever to discover the open sea. I had come to the conclusion that the only hope was to learn from Hugh's example and to renounce all worldly possessions and ambitions; in other words to join him in a bare Franciscan habit. But when and how? Renouncing possessions was one thing, renouncing debts another. And so far as anyone could see there was little prospect of anything but debts ever again. Then, once the moment had come and the plunge taken, what did one actually do? Tour the English countryside on the lines of St. Francis himself, owning nothing, sleeping under hedges and in barns, converting everyone one met? But how to convert them? And what precisely to? Or perhaps make use of the Mosquito and fly round the world with Hugh in it, preaching or converting, or helping those in need. But suppose Hugh turned out to be airsick? Or not to have a head for heights? Or to have difficulty in climbing in and out of the cockpit? And then what about Le Court itself? Should we throw its doors open to refugees and Displaced Persons? Or better still to jailbirds and those whom society rejects, living on equal terms with them and giving them new hope and a fresh start? Should we start a rest and discussion centre where people of different nationalities could come for a holiday to exchange and propagate ideas for world peace? Or should we give it all up and convert the house into flats?

To make things worse, no one seemed to have any more definite ideas than I had. Hugh would not commit himself one way or the other, beyond saying that he would make a special point of going into the chapel; Wendy was a mixture of wild enthusiasm and mysterious reserve; Pat, if the subject was so much as broached, could only say: 'Have a double whisky, old boy'; the others either answered 'Whatever you say,' or else proposed half a dozen irrelevant modifications. Mother and Father would no doubt have had something definite to suggest, but somehow it didn't seem quite fair to ask them. So what was there to do?

Just walk, walk, walk and hope to walk it off. And at the end of the walk call in to Greatham Church. There, surely, one would find an answer, or at least peace of mind. But such was not the case; the church seemed empty and dead, as if it were but four stone walls and a roof of slate, and I left it sadder and more confused than I had entered, to find God closer in the flowers, the stars, the sighing of the wind than in His man-made sanctuary.

As a change from walking, and when there was greater

urge than usual to let off steam, I took my Canadian axe and went down to the woods, where chaos reigned supreme, with whole stretches of fencing and hedges pulled away and left to rot, axle-deep ruts across the park, broken limbs and branches lying in profusion, even whole trees felled and not yet trimmed. Here at least was something constructive to do, and I went at it with a will, pleased to feel the swing of an axe again, and even more pleased to find that the axe could still find its mark and still keep swinging throughout the afternoon. Under its subduing influence, the flood-tide of schemes and plans slowed down and at times even halted altogether, to give place to the quieter memories of conversations with Hugh and the neighbouring clergy. But even these revealed divisions of opinion, on fundamental issues as well as on detail. One of the vicars, for instance, said that all that mattered was the Church, and that the Church was the Church of England; Hugh said that the Church was relatively unimportant, that God was not an administrator who worked through systems and organizations, but that He made known His will individually and personally, speaking to various men in various ways; to some perhaps through astrology, to others through inward voices, to others again through apparent coincidences and so on. Another of the vicars said that the thing that mattered was not which Church one belonged to, but how good a member one was of one's own Church and how tolerant one was of others; that all the various Churches and denominations were but different members of the Church of God travelling along parallel lines towards the same goal. He also said that God's special and greatest gift to man was Communion and that the Church should offer it to whoever wished to accept it, whether he be married or divorced, Methodist or Seventh Day Adventist, or not even a believer at all. But when there was talk of introducing the practice into Le Court, Wendy blew up. Did I, she asked, know what Holy Communion really was? Obviously not, or I could never have made such a monstrous suggestion. There was only one man who could put me right, her former Rector, and the sooner she sent for him the better.

Then, not long afterwards he came to see us. He was a tall, distinguished-looking man, who, on being shown the chapel, knelt down and said a prayer instead of inspecting the fittings and making some favourable comment as was the usual practice. By religion he was a 'very High Anglo-Catholic', which appeared to mean that he was as close to Roman Catholicism as it was possible to get whilst still looking down upon it as a false Church, and his main purpose in coming was to get down to business with Hugh and myself. So when dinner was over we all retired to Wendy's room to talk. The conversation started on a friendly note with Hugh kneeling on the floor, as was a favourite habit of his, playing with the tassel of his cord, and talking generally about the different attitudes in which one could say one's prayers, and other safe and non-controversial subjects. Later, Wendy's friend asked him about the work that had been done at Le Court, and his views on the future. Hugh seemed pleased at this opportunity, and stood up with his elbow in the mantelpiece and foot on the fender, holding forth for an appreciable time on the Universal Brotherhood of Man and the importance of Charity and Faith.

At intervals the Rector interrupted to ask him to be more specific. Was it enough to have faith in God alone, or must one also have faith in Christ, and what did faith in Christ imply? Then what about the Church? Was there one true Church of Christ or several? Did the Church have an official body of teaching which it was encumbent on all Christians to accept or believe? Or could one hold one's own private views? What, finally, about Hugh's own position? Did he claim to be an authorized representative of the Church, or did he justify his teachings on some other ground? As these questions developed and became more personal, Hugh tried to lead the conversation back to general principles, picking up the ornaments on the mantelpiece rather like display bottles, to illustrate the point he wanted to make. He was distinctly on the defensive, and by the time we finished, with most of the questions having gone unanswered, I was given food for thought indeed.

Next morning the Rector returned to the fray, but this time alone with myself in a quiet corner of the garden. If I was content to accept the personal views of a good and holy man, and felt that Hugh was the guide I wanted, then well and good; there was nothing more to be said. But if I was looking for the true Church of Christ and its official teaching, imparted with the authority of God Himself, I would have to look elsewhere.

Where?

To the Anglo-Catholics. The Roman Catholics had swung off the true path in one direction; the Anglicans, in an effort to counter it, had swung off in the opposite direction. Now, in the last 100 years the Anglo-Catholics had emerged as the true centre, the via media, to which all denominations must eventually gravitate; and in fact already were gravitating, for there were signs that the more far-seeing of Roman Catholics were becoming dissatisfied with the Catholic stand and were preparing to bring the rest of the Catholic Church into line with the Anglo-Catholic position. If I cared to do so, he would only be too pleased to put me up at the Rectory for as long as I liked to stay, and then we could do a full course of instruction. Moreover, there was the question of my future, and he had various suggestions he would like to make, and people he thought I ought to meet, before I committed myself too fully in any one direction.

This invitation I accepted with a full and thankful heart. At last, after all the false starts, I had found the True Church. But no, I had not. One night sufficed to show me that whatever good there might be in Anglo-Catholicism—and indeed there was much—its appeal was only to a limited few, not to the whole wide world; that its authority might satisfy some, but that speaking for myself it did not.

Deeply impressed though I was by the Rector, and

despite the authority that there undoubtedly was in Anglo-Catholicism, I found something lacking. Difficult to say exactly what, but none the less something.

And so I returned to Le Court to set the final seal on the process of liquidation, to announce an end to all thoughts of further schemes. The house would be turned into flats and rented out to help meet the debts; Pat and Wendy, since they had been good enough to offer, would stay on to supervise and manage, with George Swinden to help; the rest would have to go and make a new life for themselves. I, too, would embark on a new life. For in the post had come a surprise invitation from Winston Churchill's United Europe Movement to take part in their First International Congress to be held at The Hague in May. The fate of Europe, it was pointed out, nay, even that of all humanity, might well be decided there. It was the obvious step to take. Yes, most certainly it was. Who could tell what it might lead to?

Everything works out for the best.

Even failure.

8

THE outstanding feature of The Hague Congress, as it turned out, was its naked and unashamed agnosticism. The new Europe of its fashioning was to be a political, cultural, and economic entity, and nothing else. In the long and eloquently worded manifesto that was circulated to the delegates, reference was made to Europe's glorious heritage, which it was encumbent upon the present generation to acknowledge and preserve. Christianity, it is true, represented part of that heritage, but only as a thing of the past, a beautiful relic of olden days for which we, the vigorous architects of the present, must build a fitting museum for all generations to inspect and admire.

According to the Anglican clergy present, this was an attitude of mind to be opposed by every means at their disposal. Christianity alone had salvaged civilization from the ruins of the Dark Ages, and in Christianity alone was there hope for the future. But for all their indignation and insistence that something be done, the clergy did not feel prepared to stand up on the platform and force the issue themselves; they thought it would be better if it were to come from a layman, leaving them as a kind of mobile reserve to fill up the gaps and deal with the opposition. Yet when it came to the point and a layman had been found to play his part, they themselves remained where they were, glued to their seats. Neither was there any support from the Catholics or Nonconformists. On the last day but one of the Congress, the clergy's spokesman did actually get to his feet, but only to say: 'Let us ensure that those building the new Europe be imbued with strong Christian and Spiritual values.' The Chairman, his chief antagonist, was on him like an eagle: 'Why Christian and Spiritual? Do you mean that Christian is not Spiritual? Or that it covers only a part of spirituality? Or what?'

There was an uncomfortable pause. 'I'm afraid that I must refer that question to the sub-committee.'

Better, one would have thought, not to have stood up at all than to have squinted one eye over the top and then hurriedly withdrawn it at the sound of the first bullet. Yet, on second thoughts, no. Better that we who listened should know where we stood, that it should be made abundantly clear that what we were witnessing—whatever else it might be—was not Christianity. For Christianity, to be authentic, must conform to its name, it must speak as Christ spoke, and Christ spoke with authority, so much so that the crowds marvelled and that his enemies were reduced to silence. He was the witness *par excellence* who spoke of what was known to Him and testified to what His eyes had seen. A witness who testifies to what he has heard and seen neither prevaricates nor hesitates, nor is he unbalanced by cross-examination. He is there neither to explain nor to defend, but simply to state. Such was the way of Christ in the face of opposition; such must always be the way of His Church; but such was not the way of the clergy at The Hague. Yet to be fair the clergy were in a dilemma. The cause they had come to uphold was not just the Christianity of their own particular denomination, nor even that of the Church of England as a whole, but Universal Christianity versus materialism. Scattered throughout the room were Christians of every sort and description, widely differing in their view and beliefs, and anxious to preserve the integrity of their own particular denomination. No doubt with careful phrasing and thought a formula of Christian belief could be evolved that would satisfy the needs of the moment and be acceptable to at least the majority. But what if the formula should be challenged by the opposition, and they be called upon to define exactly what they meant by a Christian? How then would they answer without driving a wedge between themselves? True, they could say: 'One who believes in Christ and acts upon that belief,' but the opposition would hardly let it pass at that. And then what? If they said: 'One who believes Christ to be truly God and truly Man', a section of the room would protest this was going too far. Yet if they said less than this, another section would object they were not going far enough, that they were lowering Christianity to a purely human institution. If they approached it from a different point of view altogether and said: 'A member of this, that or the other Church or of any number of Churches,' someone would ask: 'What about me, or Jones, or anyone you like, who does not believe in organized religion, but still looks up to Christ as a good and great man and tries to follow His teachings?' And if in order to present a united front they should all agree to accept this lowest common denominator as an adequate definition, they would then have conceded the victory to the opposition; for could they not justly reply: 'If that is all you mean by Christianity, then why all the fuss; why the necessity for the Church? For don't we all look upon Christ as a good man? Aren't we all trying to put His teachings into practice in our individual ways? Have *you* any better right than the rest to lay down the law and speak in His name?'

The recognition that there was a gap in our defences found a place in many of the clergy's hearts and, in the intervals between sessions, the problem was discussed and the plans of campaign were prepared. The need for reform, for modernization, for a return to the ancient simplicity of the Faith, for Disestablishment, for public penance and for countless other similar remedies, was variously pleaded. But without, at the end of the Congress, any tangible result. Only one of the clergy present, a high official in Lambeth Palace, struck me as having a constructive and fighting approach, and so to him I now turned. He had a plan of campaign to propose to me personally—once, that is, Le Court's affairs were settled and I was free to go wherever I would. But back at Le Court, there was an unexpected development. Wendy greeted me at the front door with the news: 'Arthur is very ill. He's in hospital and asking to see you.'

Arthur. The name was vaguely familiar, but what with the unexpectedness of Wendy's outburst and the many questions I wanted to ask about Pat's progress in converting Le Court into flats, I could not for the life of me think who Arthur was. Then the light slowly dawned. I remembered an old man who used to feed the pigs and who had never been known to speak on his own initiative. Wendy was eyeing me with some disapproval, and then began to mention the word 'cancer'. Cancer! The very word itself made me feel embarrassed and ill at ease, for if there was one thing I dreaded it was finding myself alone with someone who was dying. Sick beds, I intimated, were not quite my line, and would be far better attended to by a woman. If it were a question of needing money or help of a practical nature, then naturally I would do anything in my power, but as for going in person and seeing him, well, after all I hardly knew the old boy and the only time I'd ever done any hospital visiting was to smuggle in a bottle of whisky to Charlie Whitworth, my first flying instructor, who had mistaken the edge of a roof for a puddle in the blitz, stepped off it and broken his leg. And that kind of thing wouldn't be quite appropriate under the present circumstances.

But no, Wendy was adamant, and her stare unyielding.

So, a few days later, I went. I bought some fruit and some flowers, and pulling myself together as best I could reported to the hospital. To my surprise I was told that Matron wanted to see me in her office. She explained that Arthur was suffering from an incurable cancer, and that since the hospital was only a small one with a great shortage of beds he could not stay there any longer, for they needed his bed for others who could respond to treatment. Would I, therefore, accept responsibility for him and find somewhere for him to go, for he had no known relatives and could give no address other than Le Court?

Well, put like that what could one do? One couldn't very well leave the old boy stranded, especially if he wasn't wanted in hospital. And, after all, he *had* served in the Air Force during the war. Yes, one must do something—though exactly what, heaven alone knows. Talk it over with Arthur first, presumably, and then ring up a doctor.

Arthur, however, never so much as gave me the chance of raising the subject at all. He said that he was now practically cured, and that he was negotiating the purchase of a small prefabricated bungalow, which he intended erecting on a convenient site in the district as soon as he got news of his discharge; if only they would tell him when that would be. I did my best to dissuade him, but he only protested he was more than capable of looking after himself, and having reached his middle seventies he wanted nothing better than to retire peacefully into a little corner of his own where he wouldn't be a nuisance to anyone else. Couldn't I, he asked, use my influence with the hospital authorities to make them give some definite news? And, more important still, wouldn't I let him have a tiny piece of land on the Le Court estate? Le Court was the only home he had had in forty years. He loved it, in spite of all the troubles of the past, and there was nothing he could ask for better than to end his days there. This was a decidedly awkward situation, and on my way out I called in to see the Matron to ask whether Arthur had been told about his condition. She answered very indignantly 'No,' adding that such a procedure would not only aggravate his condition, but was entirely contrary to medical practice. Moreover, it was incumbent on me to conform to hospital policy and not say anything that would give the secret away. That settled it.

A day or two later, having plucked up my courage, I returned for a second visit. I neither called to see Matron nor asked permission from anyone but walked straight into

Arthur's room. He was not there. Finally I found him sitting in a kind of miniature verandah which looked out on a narrow strip of lawn. He was bundled up in blankets, in spite of the warm May sunshine, and looked if anything frailer than the last time. Yet his eyes were steady and firm, rather as those of a man who is waiting and expectant. I beat about the bush long enough to smoke a cigarette and to recover from the shock of having crossed the threshold; and then I came to the point. 'Arthur, I'm afraid they don't think there is anything they can do to help you.' He looked at me for further information. 'In other words, they don't think you are going to get better.' His reaction was not at all what I had expected. His eyes wandered across the lawn to the blank boundary wall in front of us, then turned slowly back to look me full in the face.

'Thank you, Len. It's a relief to know where I stand.'

That was the first time he had ever called me 'Len', but it sounded so natural, and I felt pleased and grateful. The tension was gone. I settled back in my chair, lit another cigarette and we began to discuss the next step. He had felt all along that something was not quite right, he was not really wanted in hospital—well, not exactly that, because they couldn't possibly have been kinder to him, but as if he oughtn't to be there and was imposing on their generosity. But he didn't want to leap out of the frying-pan into the fire; he was more than willing to go somewhere else, but we'd have to be careful where it was—not a hospital or an institution, but some place where he could look after himself and not be a burden. Yes, that is what was wrong, he was being a burden to other people, who already had quite enough to do as it was. I *would* promise, wouldn't I, not to let him get in that situation again? Yes, now that I saw the problem, indeed I would.

But things turned out very differently from what I had expected. Far from being any question of picking and choosing, there was not so much as an inch of floor space in a public ward, or even a fireplace sofa in a private house. Neither the National Health Service, nor any of the Benevolent Funds, whether private or public, nor any form of Home, Institution or even asylum that we could find, other than the £10-a week-and-up Nursing Homes, offered so much as a glimmer of hope. As a last resort I wrote to the County Medical Officer of Health, but all that came back in return was an instruction to re-apply in six months' time.

It was this letter that galvanized Wendy into action. She was in the midst of papering her future attic bathroom, in preparation for the day when Le Court would be turned into flats and she and Pat installed under the gables as caretakers, and, having read the letter through twice, stamped her foot on the (already rickety) floor, said: 'Well, I'll be ——' then changed her mind and burst out laughing, walked across to the window (which opened on to an almost limitless vista of lawns and wood and rolling fields), and with an abrupt wheel-about said:

'I'll look after him if you'll provide the room and a bed.'

'Will you really?' for I was much taken aback, to say the least.

'Of course I will. Would you expect anything else? Do you think we can just leave him to rot, when there's twenty-five empty rooms in this house and no prospect of any tenants coming in for simply ages—not when you consider the appalling state of all the rooms and poor Pat doing nothing but asking how he's expected to get the repairs done without any money at all.'

'Yes, but I'm planning to go away and leave Le Court—probably for good. The Padre I met at The Hague has some plan up his sleeve for me, and whatever it is certainly it won't involve my staying here, so I want to get the house fixed up and off my hands altogether. Surely you don't mean to take on Arthur under those conditions, do you? And the hospital said he might linger on for anything up to eighteen months.' But Wendy was not to be shaken.

The following morning early I went to Arthur and put the proposition to him—rather diffidently, for Le Court, in its present condition, was not exactly the sort of place one would recommend to a dying man, even allowing for all the trouble that Wendy would undoubtedly take to make up for it. But Arthur was hardly listening. His eyes were shining and dancing. 'Do you really mean it, Len?' He seemed to sigh as he said it.

'You see when I was a young boy I became a Catholic and somehow it wasn't easy to stay at home after that, so I left. And ever since then I have never had a home, not until I came to Le Court. And now you're inviting me back. It's like beginning all over again.'

Back at Le Court, however, there were signs of trouble. Pat was pacing up and down the front drive waiting to see me, evidently with a lot to get off his chest. Much as he sympathized, much as he would like to help, he would have nothing at all to do with the proposal. For one thing, Wendy was not in particularly good health, she had a large attic flat to decorate and look after, the meals to cook and a home to provide for her daughter during the holidays; it was out of the question to expect her to take on the full time commitment of a dying man, who, for all one knew, might go on living for another two years. For another thing, the presence of a cancer patient in the house would put paid for ever to the hopes of finding tenants for the flats. All true, of course, and hard to contradict.

But true or untrue, the fact remained that Arthur had been promised a home in Le Court and that he was now lying in bed counting the minutes until we came to fetch him. And, come Hell and high water, fetched he must be.

There was a kind of rushing sound from the direction of the stairs, and a breathless Wendy appeared, running at such a speed that it was all she could do to stop in time to avoid a head-on collision.

'Oh, Leonard, dear, you do understand, don't you? Do tell me that you do. You know that I really did mean it, but that I just hadn't thought of it from Pat's angle, don't you? And, of course, he's absolutely right. He usually is. But I'm so hot-headed; I never stop to think. And neither do you, do you? You've decided to look after him yourself, haven't you? Oh, but the smell.'

'The smell, Wendy? What smell? I do wish you wouldn't shoot about from one subject to another quite so quickly.'

'Arthur's.'

'Arthur? But Arthur doesn't smell.'

'He will. Don't you worry. He will—you see, Leonard dear. I had an aunt who died of cancer of the liver, just like Arthur. Oh, she was such a long time in dying. And I used to go and sit by her and help change her pyjamas when they got dirty. I can't tell you what the smell was like. It haunts me to this day. And Arthur will be just the same. You wait.'

9

WITH Arthur scheduled to arrive in only three days' time, Le Court was thrown into a certain amount of panic. Wendy, by special concession from Pat, offered to help distemper and paint the room, and shot round the neighbourhood collecting a bed, bedding and other sick-room necessities to replace those that had been sold. George Swindin, the one other surviving member of V.I.P., undertook to sell flowers from the garden so as to raise extra money. In fact he seemed suddenly to have come into his own, and was to be seen darting about here and there, now with a duster, now with a broom, now with a surprise cup of tea to revive the flagging distemperers. Finally, he waylaid me on the upstairs landing, looking for all the world as if he were the family butler and had been for years and years and years.

'A'hm. Very likely you'll be looking for a nurse.'

'A nurse! No, certainly not; that's the last thing we want. If there's anything to be done for Arthur, we'll do it ourselves. In any case it's out of the question, we can't afford it.'

'Ah, yes, of course.' George's manner indicated that all this was properly expressed, very properly indeed—so far as it went.

'But very possibly there might be certain advice that a nurse could give.' He almost said 'Instruction', but held himself in check just in time. 'As, for example, on the subject of haemorrhages, stoppages of the bladder, incontinence, bouts of vomiting, looseness of the bowels, swooning fits. . . .'

'Good God, George, we haven't got to expect that kind of thing, have we?'

'Only a precaution . . . of course. But, seeing this is my evening off—in a manner of speaking, that is—and that a young lady of my acquaintance is coming to see me, who happens to be a trained Sister, I thought that a few minutes' conversation might be beneficial.' And beneficial, indeed, they turned out to be.

Beginning with a general talk about such rudimentary matters ('and obviously you know all about *them*, but we might as well start at rock bottom') as blanket baths, draw-sheets, pressure points, hospital corners, donkeys, and other similar terms of everyday use, and having revealed an abysmal ignorance in their respect, we settled down to a systematic course of instruction designed to cover the entire gamut of nursing in three consecutive evening classes. We started with pure theory, proceeded to what the Air Force would call a dummy run, and concluded with a full scale operation with George as primary target—or perhaps one should say dummy.

First we administered a blanket bath, by which is meant (*a*) that the entire body is scrubbed from head to foot MORNING AND EVENING; (*b*) that never at any given moment is more than five square inches of skin exposed to atmosphere (so as to avoid danger of chill, shock or embarrassment to the patient), and (*c*) that the whole manœuvre is completed rapidly enough for the water to remain as hot at the end as it was at the beginning, even on a bitter winter's day. Next we changed the bottom sheet with the dummy in the bed, and this by dint of rolling him to the extreme edge as if he were a log, then preventing him, by sheer physical force, from either falling off or regaining occupancy of the centre; then ripping out the sheet from the free side of the bed and instantly replacing it with a clean one; then reversing the process with the utmost speed and dexterity; then restoring the whole ensemble to its pristine calm and order. All without pausing for breath. Finally we went to work with a bedpan. For a full fifteen minutes (the patient, by explicit instructions, being inert and incapable of co-operating) we heaved and we pushed and we levered, at times even resorting to deft (but sharp) nips and pinches, until eventually we succeeded. When, at long last, George was sitting back against the pillows, his few strands of hair standing up in a little tuft and with a kind of breathless and strained expression on his face, the Sister Tutor said:

'You now turn to the patient and say: "Are you comfortable?"'

'And what if he should say NO?'

'He never would. He'd never dare say that; not to a nurse.'

But Arthur appeared to have no such inhibitions in regard to those who were appointed to look after him. He scorned the suggestion of being put into an ambulance, and had to be fetched in the Standard Eight that Father had recently given me. He poured a withering look on Wendy when she rushed forward from the front door pushing the wheelchair and murmuring: 'Poor Arthur; poor Arthur,' and staggered painfully into the house under his own steam. He resolutely and defiantly resisted all attempts to carry him up the stairs. He refused point-blank to have any truck with blanket baths, bedpans, or even commodes and bottles, and instead had to be slowly (and very frequently) escorted to the bathroom and lavatory. Only when, on first entering the room, he caught sight of the log fire did he show any sign of pleasure, but even that did not last very long. Last thing at night, before taking final leave of him, I timidly pointed to a long piece of wire hanging from the ceiling. It was the bell-pull that had been dismantled from the back door and precariously re-installed between our respective bedrooms.

'All you've got to do, Arthur, if you want anything in the night is to pull it.'

'Thanks, Len, all the same, but I shan't want it. In fact, if it weren't so difficult to get at, I'd ask you to take it away here and now. Still, it was very good of you to think of it. Very good indeed.' And so to bed.

In the middle of the night—that is to say at the precise moment when sleep is deepest and dark most impenetrable —the bell rang. It rang and rang and rang. It simply would not stop ringing. My bedroom was directly over the crack in the foundations, so that the floor sloped steeply away towards the fireplace. In the confusion of leaping out of bed, I knocked the matches off the broken chair that served as a bedside table; then no sooner did I put the chimney of the lamp on the floor when it rolled away down hill out of reach and worse still out of sight. But still the bell kept pealing. Through my head ran George's words of warning—haemorrhages, swooning fits, sickness; and much else that the young nurse herself had touched on in odd moments of relaxation between exercises. I saw visions of a dying man, of fountains of blood, of convulsive fits, of heaven knows what, and then, at long last, having finally managed to light the lamp, I rushed at the door, remembering just in time to walk in as if nothing were of the slightest consequence and the whole situation entirely under control. Arthur was sitting sedately up in bed with just a slightly worried expression on his face.

'Len,' he said, 'it's a cat. I simply can't bear cats and one's just jumped in through the window and walked across the foot of my bed. And to tell the truth, it doesn't seem like an ordinary cat at all. Ah, Len, I'm not feeling as well as I had hoped. Perhaps, after all, I shall need a little help.'

In the last week of June I asked Arthur a point-blank question. It had been at the back of my mind for several days, and more than once I had been on the point of putting it to Pat and Wendy; but somehow I had never quite managed to get it out. In any case it was so intimately connected with Arthur, so much part and parcel of the extraordinary way in which he had settled so happily into Le Court, in spite of its rigours and shortcomings, that it seemed almost a breach of confidence to put it to anyone else. So one evening, in a lull after supper, I asked him straight out:

'What do you think of cancelling the flat idea, and turning Le Court into a home for people like you—er—I mean, people who haven't anywhere to go and can't look after themselves?'

The question did not seem to take Arthur by surprise at all, and he seized on it eagerly. 'Yes, Len, I think we ought to do it. I think God wants us to. And I think I could help you too.'

'*Help* me? . . . Oh, yes, of course, I see what you mean. But how were you able to answer so quickly? Had you been thinking about it before, or was it just a sudden inspiration?'

'Neither really—or I suppose I should say, a bit of both. I hadn't actually thought of *that* idea at all, but I *did* feel that God couldn't have sent you along at that particular moment just for *my* good, and I was . . . well, sort of expecting some development. I rather felt you were, too; you looked rather lost.'

'Lost. But that's ridiculous. I wasn't feeling lost, in fact just the contrary. As a matter of fact there have been times in the past when I have felt rather lost, but I've just had the good fortune to come across a most excellent Padre in Lambeth, who's becoming my spiritual director; and what with a letter of advice and instructions from him every week and a weekly session with the Vicar—though admittedly they don't always see eye to eye on everything, but still that's only a minor detail—I've never been better placed. So you were quite wrong there.'

'Probably I was. Anyway it's really rather beside the point. The point is; how are we going to find the sort of people we are looking for? We can't very well advertise ourselves as a nursing home.'

'Well, I hadn't actually looked as far ahead as that. In fact I don't really think we ought to take any action at all—just leave it in the hands of Providence and see what happens. If anyone turns up, we take them. If no one turns up, we write the idea off and let Pat continue with the flat scheme. Then, if patients come, we won't have to worry about not having any money, will we? We turn round to Providence and say: "We haven't asked for them; so may we please have some money?"'

'Yes, Len, that's quite right.' Arthur looked almost excited and began warming up to his subject.

'But are you prepared to accept anyone who turns up, no matter who they are—I mean assuming they are genuine, of course? Because you can't have it both ways, you know. You can't very well accept the money God sends, unless you also accept the patients He sends. I mean if you're not going to run round and refuse a cheque because it's too large—which you're not, are you?—can you in good conscience turn round and refuse a patient just because he's too difficult or you're too busy? Assuming, of course, that he really hasn't got anywhere else to go. And that goes for the helpers, too—for everything, in fact. If you're going to leave the initiative to God, you'll have to be consistent. Is that what you intend?'

'Oh, yes, I'm quite prepared for all that. After all, it goes without saying, doesn't it?' Arthur looked pleased and satisfied; he nodded his head.

But such could not quite be said of the others, and first reactions were very mixed. Wendy alternated rapidly between saying that it was the most wonderful idea she had ever heard of (and oh, how she did hope it would come off) and asking how on earth I managed to get so many extraordinary and utterly impractical schemes into my head. Pat looked, and was, positively horrified. George answered that he was more than ready to fall in with whatever was decided. Father brought the full weight of his command of English to bear and, with all a parent's solicitude for his erring son, pleaded with me to reconsider. Mother maintained a discreet silence. Aunt Edith, fortunately, knew nothing about it. The Vicar preferred not to commit himself one way or the other, but did take the trouble to come and hold a small dedication service to help us along whatever path we might finally choose. My Spiritual Director, after urging caution and writing some most edifying letters on the spiritual life, came down to see for himself, and arrived at the conclusion that the plan was ill-advised.

'Your situation [he wrote] is very like that of a man of magnificent physical powers who has not learnt to run properly and therefore is unlikely to win any races except those of a markedly inferior standard—your spiritual capacity is, so to speak, not in training. I suggest that you should not accept the help which you tell me has unexpectedly been offered you; that you give up completely all the plans you have thought about, and that in fact you detach yourself from them, and concentrate on the development of your spiritual life . . . you have still to learn the real submission to the Will of God.'

In saying that I was in need of spiritual training and discipline he was undoubtedly right, and I could not help but admit it in my answer. But could it not, I asked, equally well be acquired in a work of charity as in a vacuum? In fact was it not, perhaps, an act of selfishness to turn away a man who asked for help on the grounds that one had to attend to one's own soul? Moreover, the offer of help was not so easily disposed of as that. It had originated with a surprise visit from the Marchioness of Cholmondeley, whom I had recently met in London. She had come down to see for herself what was going on, bringing with her a Fortnum and Mason's hamper of just the sort of things that Arthur could eat; and for a full hour she had sat on Arthur's bed talking to him and putting him at his ease.

'Le Court,' she subsequently wrote, 'has succeeded in making one old man happy without exactly giving him *luxury*, and I don't see why it shouldn't do the same for many others, too. I wouldn't let anyone on earth talk you out of it.'

And just to reinforce her letter with action she had rung up to say she was sending a pantechnicon full of 'odds and ends of furniture—beds, chest of drawers, and so on', adding that if we found they were no use at all perhaps they would fetch a few pounds at a sale. Then, after a fortnight of torment, torn between respect for the clergy and the urge to open Le Court's doors to the sick and homeless, and hoping to find, if not guidance, at least peace of mind, I ran into the room that served as a chapel and opened the Bible at random. It read: 'Trust ye not in a friend.'[1] I wrote off at once to Lambeth and said that I had come to a decision. I would remove, so far as possible, all preconceived plans and ideas from my head, and as calmly as I could commit the future into the hands of Providence, neither looking for patients nor refusing them if they should appear of their own accord, and being equally content whichever way it should turn out.

Yet even this was not enough to still the conflict and the doubts, which raged and stormed until at one stage I thought that I would be literally sick. Fortunately time was limited and work plentiful, or else I might well have given up in despair. There was breakfast, tea and supper to be produced—George did the lunch—the wing of a house to sweep and dust; the daily ablutions to preside over; pyjamas to wash, increasingly more and more often; bells to answer in the night; companionship to provide for Arthur and long evening discussions on religion or the future in general. Above all, there were debts to settle, negotiations for the sale of the cottages and estate to be completed, accounts to pore over with Cyril Cowey, erstwhile book-keeper of V.I.P., who called in each day on his way home from work.

Then there was the condition of the house. It had been due for a coat of paint at the beginning of the war, but the wartime prohibition on building and decorating had prevented it being done. The outside woodwork, of which there was a great deal, looked decrepit and haggard, and in parts had

[1] Micah vii, 5.

124

begun to rot. The eighty-odd windows, all of which (except the attic) were huge, had broken their sashes and were permanently either jammed shut or wedged open. The flat lead roof over the hall, which even in its heyday had been liable to surreptitious leaks, was now in the habit of syphoning torrents of water down the staircase, to the detriment of the once-majestic wallpaper and to the encouragement of a colourful variety of fungi. The chimneys, all of them sixty feet above ground level and more, were choked with soot, or perhaps jackdaws' nests, and ridiculed the attempts at amateur sweeping. The once highly polished parquet floors were black and glutinous from successive layers of dirt, polish, more dirt and more polish.

Old Waghorn the builder, whose stature was unbelievably small but his moustache unbelievably large, and who for nigh on twenty years had visited Le Court in the same rickety green-coloured van, on being called upon for a professional opinion, gave vent to a succession of long and reproachful sighs, and confided that £1,000 would barely cover the bottom of the bottle.

£1,000! And our total assets were 27s. per week from Arthur's Old Age Pension and whatever George could raise from the sale of fruit and vegetables—now his chief occupation.

Then there were the lawns, the full acre and a quarter of them, of every conceivable size, shape, and contour. In Aunt Nancy's day they had been the pride and glory of the district, shorn and edged as if in perpetual preparation for a bowls tournament or an At Home. Now they had run wild—in parts even indistinguishable from the neighbouring fields—except immediately opposite the sun porch where Pat, with the daily use of a hand mower (which no one else was allowed to touch) was keeping a small green patch under faultless control.

The motor-mower, which had seen its prime during the war and suffered atrocious treatment at the hands of

V.I.P. had been pushed into the potting-shed and had lain forgotten throughout the winter. It was now dug out, reluctantly roused to life by the persistent efforts of a neighbouring motor-cycle mechanic, and turned loose on the grass. Pat, who had spent the better part of his sporting days on a golf course and who had once had a handicap of two, was appalled and shocked:

'I say, old boy,' he said, 'mowing machines aren't meant for hayfields, you know. I mean, there are limits.'

But sink or bust the hay had to be reduced to a lawn, and how else was it to be done? So by dint of a running start and a wide open throttle and a fair proportion of elbow grease, battle was joined. At times the chain came off, or broke; at times the engine gave up the unequal fight and was abandoned on the touch-line until the mechanic could spare time to come and attend to it; at times the blades were outmatched by the length of the grass and had to give way to a good old-fashioned scythe or sickle. But slowly and surely the perimeter retreated; the area of resistance narrowed.

One evening, down by the peonies, when tackling the toughest piece of all (mainly because of a mass of fallen twigs and hazel husks which were intertwined with the grass), there was a piercing cry, and I turned round to find Cyril holding his nose and prancing round in circles, repeating: 'That hurt. That hurt.' Cyril, it may be said, was everlastingly being overtaken by some calamity or disaster otherwise unheard-of in anyone else's life, but on this occasion he had gone one better even than usual—he had trodden on the rake. 'Good heavens, Cyril! I thought that only happened on films.'

'Well, if it happens on films like it does in real life, I shouldn't like to be an actor. You're wanted on the telephone, and you'd better be quick, it's from London; and for the first time in history, the books balance.'

Cyril had an incurable habit, when under stress, of speaking very rapidly and of stringing a whole series of unconnected ideas into one sentence.

'Is this a joke?'

'No, it's *not*—any more than a rake is.' Peals of laughter, fading into the distance, as I ran off.

The call was an unusual one—from Reg Wilkins, the porter at Aunt Edith's block of flats, in whose basement kitchen I had drunk many cups of tea on my way upstairs, and on occasions spent the night on a rug on the floor. But for Reg to telephone must mean some unusual or startling news. Possibly Edith had heard what was going on and was on her way down to see for herself. But Reg meanwhile was talking six to the dozen. He had a grandmother-in-law who was ninety-one. She had been bedridden—or virtually so—for eighteen months. She lived in a fourth-floor flat—well, hardly a flat, but anyway on the fourth floor. Her husband had just had a stroke and had been taken off to hospital. She was alone. The wife—Reg's that is—took her up some food as often as she could, but it wasn't exactly easy, she living in Hammersmith— the grandmother-in-law, that is—and they living at Wilton Place and having all the flats to see to. There just wasn't anywhere for Granny to go to. Nowhere at all. Well, after hearing from my aunt about what was going on at Le Court (unprintable some of it) the wife and he had wondered . . . only wondered, of course . . . whether we could take her?

What, we could? Really! Without even filling up a form, or sending a reference. . . . Oh, sheets. Yes, she could bring her sheets and blankets. . . . When? Well, the sooner the better. Yes, the sooner the better. It was very urgent. . . .

The following afternoon, almost immediately after lunch, Granny arrived. She came in a fully fledged L.C.C. ambulance with two uniformed drivers in attendance, and was carried into the house on a stretcher with all the usual hospital routine and trappings. She was generously swathed in blankets, dressed up to the nines and wore on her head a saucer-shaped hat from which protruded a single enormous feather. Her face was small and wizened, but alert and inquisitive. As the cortège passed through the porch and got into its stride, the feather responded by waving in rhythm with the ambulance men's step. But on entering the inner hall, with its drooping wallpaper and its vast expanse of empty unpolished parquet floor, there was evidently a hitch, for the cortège came hesitatingly to a halt, and a query was raised as to whether or not there had been some mistake about the address. The necessary assurance being duly given, the cortège once more proceeded on its way. It mounted the long, broad oak stairs—a squad of Guards could hardly have done better, nor raised a louder echo—and wheeled abruptly left at the top to enter what in former days had been the principal guest room, and was now empty except for a dilapidated iron bedstead, a mattress, a folding chair, an ex-Y.M.C.A. card table, and a hastily arranged vase of flowers. Here there was a further moment of hesitation; the ambulance men, it seemed, had anticipated something slightly different; moreover they were looking expectantly round as if waiting for someone to arrive and take command. They were assured there was no one else to come and were asked whether they had remembered to bring the sheets. 'The sheets. Oh, yes . . . the sheets. Ha, ha, ha.' This seemed to break the ice, for they suddenly became perfectly ordinary human beings, and Cockneys at that; they pushed their caps back on their heads, relieved themselves of their feelings (fairly mildly) and having put the stretcher down and taken off their jackets, rolled up their sleeves in preparation for some work.

'She's a real character is Granny,' they confided, once the proceedings of getting her into bed were under way. 'Practically stone deaf, except on occasions when she wants something special, eyesight none too good, but never misses a thing; can't do a thing for herself, apart from when she wants to make things real difficult for you, and very particular about her food. But once you get the hang of it, it won't be too bad. Never is, not when you get the hang of it. That's all you've got to do, Guv'nor, get the hang of it.'

But getting the hang of Granny was not as simple as one

might have supposed. In the first place she was not practically stone deaf, but completely so, with the result that one could only make oneself understood by approaching very close to her ear and bawling at the top of one's voice. In the second place she was distinctly limited in her topics of conversation, the two main ones being to the effect she wished to be taken home immediately and please what had happened to her cat? Occasionally, if she couldn't think of any better way of confusing the issue, she would beckon with her finger and say: 'Are you me 'usband?' then refusing to be satisfied until a full thirty minutes had been spent in establishing our real relationship. In the third place there was the crucial matter of the daily wash. Granny had come dressed, and other than what the ambulance men had succeeded (with great difficulty) in removing, she intended to stay dressed. In particular she was prepared to go any lengths rather than remove her stockings, which had already been on no one could guess how many weeks.

Had Arthur only had the grace to consent to be blanket bathed, all might have been well, but the nine-weeks' interval since my course of tuition had driven everything out of my head except certain isolated instructions such as: 'Test the temperature of the water by dipping your elbow into it,' 'Ask the patient whether he would prefer to do his face himself?' 'Don't get the face-flannel mixed up with the back flannel', 'Stream the patient's feet well by holding them over the bowl and squeezing water on to them from a sponge'. Even so, the position might still have been retrievable were it not for the fact that Granny had been a District Nurse in her day (though whether such nursing officials actually existed in those distant days is open to doubt), and upon the appearance of the bowl and flannel immediately switched over to a policy of so-called collaboration. No sooner was the soap put down for the fraction of a second than it was picked up and buried somewhere in the sheets; no sooner was one hand in the process of being dried than the other would set to work rearranging (and muddling up) the blankets; no sooner did I bend down momentarily to re-charge the steadily cooling temperature of the water than the just-dried hand was plunged back into the bowl, and we were back where we started. And so life continued for fourteen long days.

At lunchtime on the fifteenth day there was an unexpected development. While I was in the act of handing her her customary bowl of milk pudding, she flung her arms round my neck and kissed me. Her grip was remarkably strong. I was caught off balance. The milk pudding dropped on to her lap. 'I love you,' she suddenly croaked. Her grip around my neck was still strong, and at least I was conveniently close for the purpose of making myself understood.

I shouted out at the top of my voice: 'Well, I love you.'

'Do you love an old lady?'

'Yes, I do.'

'Well, I love a young man.'

On the morning of August 19th Arthur met with an accident. For some time now he had been too weak to walk down the passage, so a commode had been put behind a screen in his room, and each morning he staggered the eight or nine steps to reach it, painfully leaning on my shoulder. Now, halfway back to the commode, he suddenly stiffened and stood rooted to the floor. There seemed nothing to do but to pick him up and carry him into bed, but instead of letting himself go, he straightened his legs and resisted. Perhaps I should have stopped, but having begun the movement it was difficult to arrest it, and so I carried on. As I got him into my arms he shuddered and cried out: 'Lumme.' It was a cry of agony. I carried him the two remaining steps to the bed and laid him down. His head rolled to one side, and his eyes, though open, were sightless. As soon as I dared, I went downstairs and telephoned to the hospital to ask for advice. They said he had probably had a haemorrhage and there was nothing to be done; just keep an eye on him and wait. The end would probably come in a matter of hours, and then it was merely a question of laying him out. Lay him out? But surely that was a peculiar thing to do to a person already stretched out flat in bed. Ah, but I had misunderstood. Laying out was a technical expression; it was an operation that one carried out on the dead. I was given my instructions, a whole host of them, and was told on no account must I begin the operation until three hours after death.

Then I returned to Arthur. He was lying just as I had left him, but looking better, so I propped him up against the pillows and sat down to keep him company. His head had a tendency to roll on to his shoulder and his eyes to close, but at times he came to with a start and spoke quite normally. It was these periods of consciousness that I found so embarrassing and awkward, for his eyes would wander round the room with a curious, puzzled expression and then settle on me, half expectantly, as if there was something I was supposed to do or say, and the truth was that I did not know what was expected of me. Occasionally I volunteered some information about the garden; once I told him that Alf Willmot, our next patient, would be arriving the day after tomorrow, and this seemed to interest him, for he half smiled and said: 'That's good.' Once I asked him if he wanted a cigarette, but it was a foolish question, and after trying hard to puzzle it out he gave it up and fell back into unconsciousness. Suddenly he sat forward, looked straight at the fireplace and said: 'I suppose I'll have to go.' But from the way he spoke, he sounded puzzled and as if trying to make up his mind. I wondered what about. For the rest the hours passed in silence and semi-consciousness.

At three o'clock, finding inactivity too much of a strain, I called in the next-door room to exchange a few words with Granny. She was comfortably settled under layer upon layer of blankets, in spite of the season, and had an expression which said: 'Something's up. I know it perfectly well, and don't think that I don't.' Then I went out into the garden to do some mowing. The end of the grass-growing season was in sight; the lawn mower was still holding its own, even if only by the skin of its teeth. Victory was almost at hand. But it would not do to slacken the pace. Arthur himself would not want that.

When I returned at four o'clock Arthur was still unconscious, but there was a suspicion of a rattle in his throat. At half past five the front-door bell rang, and I found a middle-aged woman on the doorstep, panting heavily from the walk up the drive, and clutching an enormous basket of fruit and flowers. She introduced herself as Mrs. Nancy Mills and said she had been asked to visit the Catholic patient whom she understood we had in the house. When I broke the news of Arthur's condition she explained she had done Red Cross nursing in the war and was well used to this kind of situation, and seemed torn between two desires; the one to stay and talk and offer such help as she could; the other one to rush off and tell Father Clarke, the Parish Priest, that Arthur was dying—which, of course, was a point I had clean overlooked. In the end the latter triumphed, and after telling me that she herself had only just been discharged from hospital, but that once she had finished her convalescence she would be only too pleased to come and help—if I thought it would be any use—she left.

Arthur was now visibly sinking. His breathing was fainter, the rattle in his throat more pronounced, and his face old and strained. He was half lying, half sitting up against the pillows, but tilted over on his right side. Seven o'clock struck, eight o'clock, nine o'clock. The rattle grew steadily louder. When I wasn't thinking of the moment of death and whether or not I would ever remember the long list of instructions for laying him out, my mind wandered back over the past to the conversations we had had together, more often than not on the subject of religion. Arthur had lapsed from the practice of his religion for nearly thirty years, but had regained his faith during his first few weeks at Le Court. His peace of mind and the quiet certainty of his beliefs, in spite of his evident lack of education and instruction, had impressed me greatly. Often enough he would say: 'Len, you ought to become a Catholic, too,' and I had laughed, for was not that exactly what one would expect a Catholic to say? Was it not also an opportunity for showing him that so far as I was concerned we were all merely going in the same direction along our own individual paths, that what he believed was in essence exactly and precisely the same as I believed? Yet he had been extraordinarily obstinate about this, and when I had asked him what, in his opinion, was the difference between the Church of England and the Church of Rome, he had answered: 'The Church of England has kept the shell and thrown away the kernel.'

'And what is the kernel?'

'The Mass. . . . Ah, the peace after hearing Holy Mass.' No one who heard the way in which he spoke those words, 'Ah, the peace after hearing Holy Mass', could fail to be impressed, and from that day onwards we had argued no further.

At 11 p.m. Father Clarke arrived. He was tall and heavily built, with a ruddy complexion and black hair showing a suspicion of grey. His hands were not those of one used to manual work and I classified him in my mind as an academic rather than a man of action. As I escorted him up the stairs, I was curious to know what his reaction would be when he found himself faced with a dying man. But Father Clarke was unperturbed. He walked up to Arthur, touched his forehead with the back of his hand, and then asked for a small linen cloth to put on the bedside table. Having fetched the cloth, I hesitatingly asked if I could stay in the room while he conducted the service, and for the first time Father Clarke looked surprised. 'Of course you can stay,' he said. 'Why should you ask?'

I thanked him and knelt at the foot of Arthur's bed, while he put on his short white surplice and purple stole, lit the candles and made certain preparations on the small bedside table. I had always supposed that a clergyman's function by a deathbed was to give words of comfort and encouragement, and since Arthur was unconscious I was intrigued to know what form the service would take. It soon became clear, however, that Father Clarke had come not so much to say something as to *do* something. He began by reading a few prayers in Latin; then proceeded to anoint Arthur on the head, hands and feet, repeating further prayers for each separate anointing; finally he spoke in English. At first I confined myself to seeing if I could make out any of the Latin words, rather as if I were back at school. Then gradually I found myself absorbed in the spirit of the ceremony, until the truth dawned on me that the priest was not concerned with giving encouragement or comfort, but with the simple fact of the forgiveness of sin: 'By this Holy Unction and by His great mercy, may the Lord forgive you all those sins which you have committed. . . .' When it was all over, he said: 'To me that's the greatest comfort of being a priest. The world that can do so much for a man when he is alive can do so little when he comes to die; at that moment he forgets the world and turns to the priest, the only man who can help him.'

After he had left, Wendy came in to see how everything was going and stayed on to keep me company. Arthur hardly appeared to be breathing at all. Midnight came, and passed. Suddenly he appeared to rouse himself from his coma and gave a little sigh. I got up and bent over his face; so far as I could tell all sign of life had gone. Wendy must have noticed me hesitate, for she walked up beside me, looked closely at Arthur and nodded her head. Then she knelt down at the foot of the bed. I would very gladly have followed her example, but found myself unable to collect my thoughts for a prayer.

A moment or two later, having asked if there was any help I wanted, Wendy gave my arm a squeeze and left. It was twenty past midnight. I wandered aimlessly around the room for a moment or two trying to formulate a plan of action, and decided that the best place to wait would be the ward kitchen at the end of the corridor. But when I opened the door the draught of air caused the lamp to flare up and then almost go out, throwing a grotesque, sliding shadow across the landing. I stopped in my tracks and conveniently remembered that there was something in the room I had forgotten. I returned to Arthur's bed, removed his pillows and covered his face with a sheet. Then I drew a deep breath and made for the door once again. This time I opened it inch by inch, shielding the lamp with my arm, and by sheer will power forced my eyes to look at the floor in front of my feet. Once outside there was nothing for it but to keep on walking down the corridor, past Granny's room, to the kitchen. But what an interminable walk it was. No sooner inside than I put the lamp down on the table and dropped down into a chair facing the door. I was practically certain that I had caught sight of an object in the middle of the landing, and I hardly dared breathe.

A minute or two passed. Gradually I became aware of the alarm clock; it was ticking, ticking, ticking. Surely it had never ticked as loud as that before? As a precaution against falling asleep (but a purely fanciful fear) I set the alarm for half past three, and as a double precaution wrote the figures 3.30 on a piece of paper. Then I sat down, but bolt upright, feeling a strong disinclination to take my eyes off the door. Nothing seemed to be happening, so I cautiously sat back and felt for my cigarettes. The packet was empty.

I opened the drawers of the dresser and rummaged through them, but there were no cigarettes. Instead I found a book; and that gave me a twinge of conscience, for it had been given to me nearly a month before on the understanding that I read it, and I had not done so. I now picked it up and idly looked through it, devoutly wishing that it would turn itself into a packet of cigarettes. According to the title page it was an explanation of the author's conversion to Catholicism—'One Lord, One Faith', by Father Vernon Johnson. Better than a ghost story in the circumstances, but that was about the best one could say.

There was a resounding crack. First out on the landing. Then up in the attic. Then next door in my bedroom. What in the name of heaven could it be? Surely not just a creaking floorboard. Nor even that confounded cat on the prowl once again. Yes, Arthur had been right when he said it was no ordinary cat. It wasn't by any means ordinary. It lived in the woods by day, scavenged in the house by night, occasionally giving me the fright of my life, and had become so furtive and wild in its manner that the R.S.P.C.A. had been given orders to shoot it on sight. But even a cat gone wild could not cause a series of creaks like that, simultaneously at four different points of the compass. No, either it was the dead revisiting their haunts of the past, or else it was nerves, just nerves. In sheer desperation I leapt to my feet, picked up the lamp, and hurried down the corridor to Arthur's room. On his bedside table were lying two full packets of cigarettes. I snatched them both and returned as fast as I had come. Necessity brooks no argument, and I stifled the early promptings of conscience. What a relief it was to be able to smoke! Then I picked up the book on the dresser and began to read. That, too, was a relief, for it occupied my mind. But in the fourth paragraph I received a shock. I read:

'The supreme reason (for my conversion) was that I could not resist the claim of the Catholic Church to be the one true Church founded by Our Lord Jesus Christ to guard and teach the truth. . . . She alone possesses the authority and unity necessary for such a Divine vocation.'

For the first time in my experience someone was talking of truth and authority as the essence of religion. I read on avidly; the creaks disappeared, but Father Vernon was a long time coming to the point, and what with breaking off to make tea, or to rest my eyes, or to run through the details of the coming operation, the scheduled time of waiting was up without our seeming to have got back to the point. 3.30 a.m. The hour had struck. It was very dark and still. The hall seemed unbelievably long and tortuous under the flickering light of the lamp. On opening Arthur's door I felt a mixture of hope and misgiving. Was it perhaps all just a dream? Would I find him sitting up in bed smoking a cigarette? Or would I find some terrible change, his face all distorted and disfigured?

But no, he was just the same as when I had covered him over with the sheet three hours ago; if anything more relaxed and at peace. I put my hand on his forehead; it was cold and clammy; so at least there was no mistake about the fact of death. With that assurance I began the operation. Removing his pyjamas was comparatively simple, but underneath the pyjamas lay three tight-fitting vests and these were by no means simple.

First I tried juggling one of his arms through the arm-hole, but there is something peculiarly unmanageable about an inert and lifeless limb, and I could not succeed. Next I propped him up with my left hand and tried to pull the vest over his head with my right, but without a third hand to control his arms I found this impossible. Finally I rolled him over, thinking that it might be easier if he were lying face down. But as I did so there was a loud rattle from his throat, and I jumped back in horror thinking that he must be still alive. Once I had recovered, I sat down and thought it out. I pulled him down in the bed, stretched both his arms above his head, and tried peeling the vests off the bottom upwards. It succeeded.

But the worst of the operation was still to come. For, in order to wash, there was water to be fetched, and in order to fetch water one had to brave the slithering, dancing shadows of the hall—and this not once, but half a dozen times at least with the lamp in one hand and a full basin of water balanced in the other. For we had no jug. However, finally even this came to an end. I closed Arthur's eyes, with the help of two pennies to hold them in place, and tied the cleanest handker-chief I could find round his chin. Then I crossed his hands over his chest, and as an after-thought wound his rosary through his fingers.

At the door I turned round for a last look at him, and saw through the window a faint streak of light piercing the eastern sky.

10

THE sun was streaming through the window when I woke.
Panic. I jumped out of bed and splashed some cold
water on my face, but my eyes were heavy and un-
responsive. It was 8 a.m. Heavens above, what on earth would
Granny be thinking without her cup of tea? And Arthur?
Suppose his bell had broken and he had had a haemorrhage?
or that his pyjamas needed changing? Then the truth dawned.
Arthur was dead; he was lying under a white sheet, with a clean
handkerchief round his head and chin; and there was a rosary
wound round his fingers. But that still left Granny, and she
was very far from dead. I started up the primus, set the tray,
wondering what would be the best excuse to make to her. But
she was sitting up in bed drinking a cup of tea and looking
exactly as if I didn't exist at all. Eventually she condescended
to turn towards me:

'Forgot all about me, didn't you?'

'No; I overslept.'

'Just like me husband; that's what he was always doing.'
Granny, of course, always got the last word, even under the
best of circumstances; and these were by no means the best.
From somewhere behind the door came a discreet cough.
Ah, George. Yes, of course, I had forgotten George; that
explained the cup of tea. I began to recount the essential facts
of the night's developments, but George's expression clearly
said: 'Can't think what anyone's got to worry about; I've got

139

the situation completely under control', and it soon became obvious that he was as well informed as I was, in fact a good deal better. I had forgotten that he had spent most of his life as a butler. He enquired what time we could expect the doctor. 'The doctor?' I asked him with some surprise. 'What's the use of sending for *him*?'

'To certify death. Otherwise we'll be liable for prosecution.' The technique was familiar enough. Station warrant officers of the old school use it on newly promoted officers who aren't as familiar with King's Regulations as they should be— as I had often enough learnt to my cost. But now, as then, it was hopeless to argue; so I took the line of least resistance and acknowledged my oversight.

'In that case, George, you'd better forget the flowers for once; dress up in your Sunday best, and go out and round him up. But for heaven's sake get a move on with it.'

George needed no prompting. In a matter of minutes he was off down the drive looking for all the world as if he were a royal courier with the destiny of a nation concealed in his wallet. I watched him from the window until he was out of sight, went in to see if all was well in Arthur's room, and after wandering about aimlessly here and there, settled down to the business of Granny's morning wash.

Finally I went out into the garden to inspect the lawns, and tried my hand at the mower. But even this palled. Everything in fact seemed to pall. Back in the ward kitchen I caught sight of the paper-covered book lying on the dresser just as I had left it six or seven hours before. For want of anything better, I picked it up and read *One Lord, One Faith*. But this time it held my attention, and I read it through to the end. The clergy had told me that there is no such thing as infallible authority in religion; that all religions contain a measure of truth, some more, some less; that all are travelling together towards the whole truth and might even one day succeed in attaining it; but that none is infallible. God alone is infallible.

Yes, answers the Catholic Church, God alone is infallible.

But Christ *is* God, who came into the world 'to bear witness to the truth'. He spoke as only God can speak, so that the crowds 'marvelled' and 'His enemies dared not ask Him any more questions'. He lived as only God can live, so that no one, not even suborned witnesses, could find any fault with Him. He laid down His life rather than be false to the truth He had come to serve, and then rose again from the dead—as only God can do. Then having risen, He sent forth the Church to speak in His name and with His authority, saying: 'Going, therefore, teach ye all nations, teaching them to observe all things whatsoever I have commanded you. . . . He who hears *you*, hears *me*. He who despises you, despises me.' Is an infallible God not powerful enough to invest His Church with His own infallibility? Is He not able to protect His truth from the human shortcomings of those who speak in His name, if He attaches such importance to the knowledge of that truth?

Ah, no, the clergy say. The truth is indeed important, and it is indeed regrettable that it is not to be found in its pristine fullness in the Church today. But more important than truth is love. For God is love, and all that matters is to love Him, and our neighbour in Him.

True enough, love is all that matters. But one cannot love what one does not know. The more one loves, the more one wants to know the object of one's love; the more one knows, the more deeply one can love. To argue that it does not much matter what one believes about God, so long as one loves Him, is not to love at all, it is to destroy the very foundation upon which alone love can exist. No love without knowledge; no knowledge without certainty of truth; no certainty of truth without infallibility; no infallibility unless the Church be Divinely founded and Divinely maintained.

And such, continues the Catholic Church, is the case. When Christ declared Himself to be God, first by inference and finally, when on trial for His life, in categoric and unmistakable terms, He was not just a good man in all other respects gone wrong on this one single point. Either He was speaking the literal truth, or He was raving mad, or else He was a deceiver. For to claim to be God, the Creator and Upholder of the universe and all that it contains, when one is in fact an ordinary mortal being, amounts to nothing short of lunacy—or else fundamental malice. And in either event the trait would reveal itself, if not in the ordinary course of life, at least under stress or strain. Yet history records how Christ was subjected to stresses and strains of every sort and description—to extremes of hunger and fatigue, to cross-examination and browbeating by skilful and treacherous interrogators, to subterfuge and betrayal by his most intimate friend, finally to death by prolonged and agonizing torture. Never once did He give the least sign of weakness or indecision; out of each encounter in turn He emerged serene and unbroken, master of himself, as of those around Him, until His dying breath. Before His enemies who were seeking to destroy Him, He could ask: 'Which of you can convict me of sin?' And none of them could answer. What other man in the course of human history could publicly ask such a question? When in her turn the Catholic Church pronounces herself to be of Divine origin and constitution, the sole and infallible guardian of the teachings of Christ, the One True Church of God, sufficient for the needs of all men of all times and nations, she sets herself on a par with Christ Himself. Either she is a deceiver and a usurper, wrongfully denying all other religions their rightful place in the economy of salvation; or else she is speaking the literal truth. One or the other; nothing less. If the one, then she is fundamentally and irretrievably bad, and should be exposed for what she is; if the other, she is fundamentally and pre-eminently good, the worthy object of the love and obedience of the entire human family, whose spiritual Mother, by God's grace, she thus is.

My reflections might well have carried on throughout the rest of the morning, but they were cut short by the arrival of George, who, though still immaculately dressed, was now looking a trifle travel-worn. His expression seemed to say:

'There's no need of you really, but you had better come along just to keep up appearances.'

Outside, on the landing, was standing a small, dapper figure, evidently the undertaker, but George was unaccountably slow in effecting the introduction. My eyes were caught by a highly polished pair of black shoes, travelled upwards along a faultlessly creased blue serge suit, out of the breast pocket of which protruded a large white handkerchief, and finally settled on an infinitely mournful face, partially concealed by an enormous moustache. 'Good God,' I said, 'It's Waghorn the builder!'

'Yes, sir,' he answered in barely a whisper, producing a black bowler hat and a pair of yellow kid gloves from behind his back, and giving just the faintest trace of a sniff. 'I've come for the measurements.' George opened Arthur's door, and we moved into the room where, without, so far as I noticed, a single movement of the hand, Waghorn produced a three-foot rule, ran it over Arthur's body, and drew a sharp breath, as if he had discovered some deep and unexpected secret. The rule disappeared as mysteriously as it had come. 'You'll be wanting oak, sir, I suppose?' There was a meaningful cough from George, whose look warned me to leave everything to him; and specifications were called for. Waghorn stepped backwards from the bed, raised his voice at least two tones and recited, as if it were poetry: 'Solid oak throughout, brass screws, handles and plate—£18 18s. 6d.; the same, steel screws and fittings—17 guineas; deal with oak veneer, brass fittings— 11 guineas; the same, steel fittings—£10; plain deal throughout £8. And, in view of the circumstances,' he added, raising his bowler hat to the level of his mouth, 'we'll make an allowance of 10 per cent.'

With an air of one who is faithfully interpreting his master's wishes and yet strongly disapproves of the whole situation, George answered:

'We'll take oak, Mr. Waghorn, brass fittings, and you'll be good enough to pay special attention to the workmanship.'

George's further arrangements were equally businesslike and efficient, and the house very soon returned to a normal routine. Then, at ten-thirty on the morning of August 23rd, he, Wendy and I set out in the small Standard Eight with Waghorn's hearse in the lead to Requiem Mass at the Catholic church in Petersfield. The coffin was carried down the nave, placed on trestles at the foot of the sanctuary and draped with a black pall. Two acolytes placed a tall yellow candle and stand at each of its four corners, and Mass began. It was conducted in Latin and was completely strange. Yet its strangeness attracted rather than repelled. At the end of it Wendy leant across and said: 'It's exactly the same as ours.' In her eyes was a look of warning, as if to say: 'Don't come here again.' I wondered why. For she had always been keen on the ceremonies of the High Anglican Church, and if this was the same as those, then what harm could there be in coming to it?

The ceremony once over, there was no time to linger, for Alf Willmot the third patient, and a T.B., was due in the middle of the afternoon. The news that he was to come had filled Arthur with joy, but not so the neighbourhood, who apparently attributed to his disease lethal qualities of such magical nature that even tradesmen calling at the back door would act as carriers to whisk the infection back to their villages. As it so happened this was the first intimation I had that T.B. was infectious at all, and so I promptly took counsel from a chest physician, a specialist and my nurse. The first explained at some length that T.B. germs were highly dangerous until sterilized, that sterilization was only properly effected by steam, and that it would be nothing short of iniquitous to introduce an active T.B. into an amateur and untrained establishment. To leave him on his own in a crowded Stoke Newington tenement block of flats surrounded by children and with three flights of stairs to negotiate, of course, was perfectly all right. The specialist declared that the ideal place for disposing of sputum (which was the principal source of germs) was down the lavatory, and that some good, honest fresh air, sunlight and Dettol would do the rest. The nurse said that nothing mattered so long as no sputum was put down the lavatory, and a complete segregation was made between the T.B.'s and the others. So, equipped with this enlightening advice, I had worked out a plan of campaign.

'Out of Bounds' notices were posted at strategic points; Alf's spoons, knives and forks and crockery were treated with a generous daub of vermilion paint (to indicate that no one else was to use them) and were scheduled for boiling on the primus after every meal; his sputum, if any, was to be disposed of in the boiler when it was lit for the once-weekly bath; his washhand basin and furniture were to be treated to as liberal a solution of Dettol as the exchequer would stand. And so on.

It was shortly before tea time that the front-door bell rang. I ran down the stairs to answer it, checking over in my mind the various points of the forthcoming routine. On the doorstep I found a tall, slightly drooping figure, with one of the longest and most solemn faces I had ever seen, every square centimetre of which proclaimed some imminent and fearful catastrophe. The figure shifted slightly and said:

' 'Aemorrhage 'ill; that's what that is.'

'Haemorrhage Hill?'

Ah, the drive. Yes, I should have thought of that and arranged for him to come up in a taxi. I took his suitcase and escorted him across the hall to the foot of the stairs, where he paused, peered upwards at the towering granite pillars, and said: 'Want to kill me orf before I even get to me room, do you, Chief?'

'Come on, man,' I answered, 'It's not so bad as that. If you'd like to take your hat off and come up to your room, there'll be a cup of tea there.'

At this Alf brightened visibly, and we proceeded slowly up to his bedroom. It was the small room which had formerly been used as the chapel, and was nicely fitted out with such essential furniture as I had been able to enveigle out of the neighbourhood, with running hot and cold water (hot once a week that is), and even a vase of flowers from the garden. Alf did not seem to notice this, however; he pulled a small blue bottle out of his pocket and held it under my nose: 'Know what this is?'

'No,' I answered.

'Sputum; enough germs in there to kill a railway carriage full of people.' I left the room to fetch a cup of tea, thinking that this alone would suffice to change the topic of conversation. But I had miscalculated. On seeing the red paint on the side of the cup, Alf literally bounded from his chair. 'So *that's* it, is it. You've only brought me here to treat me like an outcast. Red paint on the cups! That's what they do to convicts—segregate them; treat 'em different from everyone else. The next thing will be 'Out of Bounds' notices on the doors. Do you know what it is to be sitting in a railway carriage just like any other human being, and then when you bring the sputum flask out, to see everyone get up and move away. One by one; that's how they do it. Like rats getting out of a sinking ship. Never look you in the eyes. No, just like rats. Slink out; that's what they do. You wouldn't like that, would you, Chief? No, you can't imagine what it's like, can you? And now you're doing the same thing, only kind of more aristocratic like. Vermilion paint. Even the name sounds kind of derogatory, doesn't it? Vermilion. No, never expected to find it 'ere; that I didn't.'

'Ah, well, if that's the way you feel, it's simple enough. No tea.' I got up and walked out with the tray, but Alf stopped me at the door.

'Come orf it, Chief. I didn't say I wouldn't drink tea; I just said I didn't like vermilion paint. No 'arm in a little bit of fun, is there?' His face suddenly broke into a huge grin, and the gloom disappeared, so that I wondered if I was speaking to the same person. For the first time I noticed that his breast pocket contained three fountain pens, an assortment of pencils, a thermometer and a watchchain powerful enough to anchor a miniature dinghy. A man of varied parts, evidently. I put the tray down, and poured out two cups of tea. But the laughter didn't last. Long before the second cups were poured out we were back on the subject of haemorrhages—of which, it appeared, Alf had many.

That evening, shortly before lights out, the door of my room opened, and in shuffled Alf dressed in an almost jaunty dressing-gown. His fight appeared to have gone, and he looked puzzled. 'Where,' he asked, 'are the staff?'

'Right here,' I answered, 'in this very room.' This seemed to stun him. He subsided into a chair, and by the time he left, one and a half hours later, was a changed man—or so he claimed. The following morning, at coffee-time, I found him down in the lounge heaping up sticks and branches in the middle of the carpet. He must have sensed my reaction, for with the air of one who has been done an injury, he said:

'But I told you I was going to help. I'm storing up firewood for winter, and when I've chopped it up I'll stack it in the kitchen to dry.'

'No, you jolly well won't; it's out of bounds.'

Alf drew himself up and opened his mouth to remonstrate. But other than a kind of splutter, nothing came out. 'Orl right, Chief, have it your own way, Chief. But, at least, let me chop firewood up inside, not out. I'm a Cockney, not a yokel. Cockneys feel out of their element in woods. They like to be inside four walls, where they feel at home. Didn't you know that?' Well, frankly, I didn't. But after all, Alf *had* kept his promise, and that stifling of whatever it was that he was going to say must have cost him a bit, and so after a certain amount of humming and hawing he was allocated the sunporch in which to do his worst. On the whole it wasn't too bad a course, for the firewood idea soon palled, and gave way to a habit of prowling systematically over every square inch of the premises—Out of Bounds excepted—and of peering into the most unexpected corners, with the consequent unearthing of a pile of broken chairs which even the versatile George had abandoned as unusable. At the sight of these Alf's expression became positively jubilant; he said he was an upholsterer by trade, and that locked up in a Stoke Newington garage he still had a trunk full of tools and stock (webbing, rexine, tin-tacks and the like) which down in the peace and quiet of Le Court he was perfectly capable of putting to good use. If I would give him leave to go home for a night and fetch a selection, which his son, Cecil, would carry for him, he would mend every chair and sofa I could smuggle into the buildings, and a good deal more besides. So home he went.

In the meantime developments of a different kind had taken place. The groping after truth had ceased; the doubts and waverings of the past were gone; in their place, a calm, in-vincible certainty. I knew that I must go to Father Clarke and ask him for instruction into the Roman Catholic Church. Then, just when I was wondering what was the best way of making the approach, he telephoned to say he had me much on his mind, in view of all that had been done for Arthur, and wondered whether I would care to drive down to the sea with him for an afternoon out and a swim. Swimming was not exactly my strong point, neither was it an occupation I associated with a Catholic priest. Nonetheless I agreed readily enough, subject, of course, to finding someone to take charge of the house— which mercifully Wendy agreed to do. At the Presbytery Father was waiting, dressed in an open-necked shirt and grey flannel trousers, and equipped with a well-stocked picnic basket, prepared for us by his mother. He remarked that the average run of people were liable to look askance if a Priest behaved like a perfectly ordinary human being, but that one must have some relaxation from time to time. And off we set.

On the way out I broached the subject of joining the Catholic Church, but met with little response. The occasion, he said, was a purely social one and had no other object than making the most of the fine and sunny afternoon, whilst changing one's religion was a serious business to be dealt with at its proper place and time. If I really meant what I said, and still felt the same way in two or three months' time, then by all means come along to the Presbytery and talk it over; but for the time being the idea was premature—probably due to the emotional strain of Arthur's death. Meanwhile I would no doubt be interested to know something of the history of the countryside through which we were passing.

The afternoon was fine and sunny enough, but it was also windy, and the wide expanse of Wittering sands, normally filled to overflowing with trippers, was empty except for an occasional group or a dog being exercised. Just to look at it was enough to make one feel cold. The sea itself felt as if it had just arrived from some Northern region, still not acclimatized to the more temperate clime of autumn in the English Channel, and reduced me to such a state of shivering and to such a colour that even Father Clarke, who was bobbing about like a porpoise, suggested that we gave it up and had a hot cup of tea. Under its reviving influence, I returned to the fray; only this time, instead of a head-on assault I crept in from the flank. There were a number of points, I said, that were puzzling me, and I would be very grateful for some advice. One was Brother Hugh's doctrine of deciding one's proper course of action by reference to signs and other similar phenomena. The answer to this, it appeared, was simple. In principle one should decide the main issues of life, and particularly one's personal vocation, by the application of reason. Everyone was born into a particular environment, with certain aptitudes and gifts, and with certain ties and obligations. It was these that should determine his choice of a career. If, for example, a poor middle-class family had saved up in order to send their son to University to study engineering, with the result they were left with very little to live on, then, in the absence of some extraordinary circumstances this son ought to become an engineer and help support his parents rather than a missionary, even though mission work was more excellent in itself than engineering.

In the normal course of events God made known His wishes through the concrete circumstances of our daily lives, which

He expected us to interpret against the background of the Church's teaching and precepts. Only in the exceptional cases did He speak through signs or inward visions, and these, even though unmistakably genuine, should be brought before the bar of reason and submitted to the judgement of a competent and holy Spiritual Director. The Catholic Faith, he said, was founded on reason, and its practice was nothing but sanctified common sense. Evidently the phrase was a favourite one of his, for as the conversation proceeded and we moved from one subject to another, he repeated it time and again, until in spite of himself the occasion ceased to be purely social, and became one of serious discussion.

On arriving back at the Presbytery, hours later than either of us had intended, we found a frantic message from Wendy: 'Come home at once. I can't manage Granny any longer.' I leapt into the Standard and drove as if she were the Bentley returned to life for a fleeting and final outburst. But Granny I found to be her normal self, if not quieter and sleepier than usual, whereas Wendy was pacing up and down the lawn in a state of great agitation. She delivered a long and telling lecture on people who ask others to hold the fort for them and then can't keep their promise about when they are coming back, and turned on her heel into the house; but this didn't quite seem an adequate explanation of the fuss, so I followed her into the hall. There she wheeled round and started a second lecture on Father Clarke and the Catholic Church. 'I suppose,' she said, 'that he has talked you into becoming a Catholic?'

I laughed; I simply couldn't help it. 'No, the other way round.'

Wendy looked positively dumbfounded. 'What, you've made him an honest Protestant?'

'Indeed I have not; but I've plunged into icy cold water; given up eight solid hours of precious time; I've listened patiently to I don't know how many historical episodes of Hampshire's past history; I've put up with rebuff after rebuff. I've spent the whole month's petrol allowance on dinner and a glass of sherry, and it was only AFTER I had said good-bye that he changed his mind and agreed to give me instruction. Even then he rammed it down my throat that I should have to have an hour a week for six months, and that only when it was all over and I knew exactly what I was consenting to could I finally say yes. In fact, worse still, he said that the Roman Catholic Church suffered quite enough already from bad and indifferent Catholics and one should not lightly think of joining it.'

Wendy put both her hands to her ears and stared at me without uttering a word as if I were the Devil himself. Then she bolted up the stairs like a bullet from a gun. Halfway round the landing she stopped, and leaned over the balustrade and shouted down:

'You don't know what you've done to us. The Catholic Church will take this place over lock, stock, and barrel and will turn the lot of us out. They always do.'

II

CHRISTMAS EVE, 1948. Reception into the Catholic Church. A day of great activity and excitement, but also of great solemnity. The morning chores to be tackled in double quick time; an extra load of wood for the fires; a special polish on the floors; a cupboard full of parcels to wrap up and label; a dozen or more last-minute cards to address; eight patients to look after. A sudden realization that there is nothing in the larder for Christmas dinner—and no money in the bank on which to draw. Then the long-awaited chime of the clock. A hurried change. A dash for the Standard Eight, and off into Petersfield.

The entry into the church. Stillness and peace, and the faint aroma of incense. A feeling of being once more at the point of call-up. Not this time in the service just of one's country, but in that of the entire human family in the war against the common enemy of man and God, against Powers and Principalities, against spiritual wickedness in high places, against the evil that is in us all.

But it is difficult to realize that it is all really true, difficult to grasp even a small fraction of its implications. There are instructions to remember and follow, a general confession to make; in the midst of composing one's mind the thought of the missing Christmas dinner obtrudes itself, but it is mercifully driven out by the familiar sound of Father Clarke's voice and a recollection of his words of some weeks back: 'Your submission to the Church does not imply in any way a denial of the graces you have received hitherto in your life. Catholicism is essentially a positive thing and refuses to deny the existence of truth in other religions, however defective they may be. Christ is the fulfilment of all partial truths and Catholicism can do no less than imitate its Founder, and so your act of submission only brings to fulfilment and perfection all your religious experience that has gone before. Always avoid the mistake so many converts make in their first enthusiasm of deriding their past and the Church they have left. Nothing alienates others more than behaviour of this sort and, after all, God is more than capable of using schismatical and heretical Churches for His purposes.'

Then hardly the 'Come, Holy Spirit . . .' over than the Profession of Faith: 'I, Geoffrey Leonard Cheshire, holding in my hand God's holy gospels, and enlightened by divine grace, publicly declare that I accept the Faith which is taught by the Catholic, Apostolic and Roman Church. I believe that Church to be the one true Church which Jesus Christ set up here on earth; to which I make my submission with all my heart.'

How victorious and triumphant it sounds! Would that one could declare it, not just before a small handful of Catholic friends, but before the whole wide world—before the friendly, the indifferent, the hostile, all and everybody alike. I, Geoffrey Leonard Cheshire, in making this, my Profession of Faith, declare that I have at long last been set free from the chains of error and doubt. I declare that I no longer have to guess at the truth about life and death—and all that lies beyond. That I no longer have to choose between this line of argument and that, between this religious denomination and the other; that I have now stumbled across the truth—the truth not as man supposes it to be, but as God knows and guarantees. And the truth has set me free. I declare that just as there is but one God and but one human race, so there is but one true Church and one true Faith; that just as God is Father of the human race, so the

Church has been appointed its Mother. I declare that were it otherwise, the forces of darkness would have finally prevailed, and the divisions of man triumphed over the oneness of God. Then would the human race remain for ever just a race, and never become, as so sublimely destined, a family, God's very own, the completion of Him who everywhere and in everything is complete.

Finally the ceremony is over. Fresh air and watery sun. Four or five people hurrying up with words of welcome and congratulation; all so sincere and obviously happy. Among them the baker's delivery man. A sudden overwhelming realization of what it means, even here on earth, to be received into such a family. Then, after a long and busy day, a stroll up and down outside the front door in search of peace and quiet. For tonight, of all nights, must not pass without due preparation. Never again will Christmas Eve be quite as this one; never again will there be first Midnight Mass to hear, and first communion to receive. Overhead just the stars silently running their course; from the surrounding trees and woods hardly so much as the rustle of a leaf. Time, one could almost suppose, has come to a standstill, halted by the approach of eternity. It is the eve of Christmas, the anniversary of the night when the world was reconciled with God and at last found peace. 'While all things were in quiet silence, and the night was in the midst of her course, Thy Almighty Word, O Lord, came down from Heaven, from Thy royal Throne and dwelt amongst us; and we saw His glory, the glory as of the Only-Begotten of the Father, full of grace and truth.' Yes, and as then in the stable at Bethlehem, so today Christ comes down from Heaven to give His peace to the world—in the Mass.

'The Catholic Religion,' had said Father Clarke, 'is the worship of God through Jesus Christ Our Lord, and it is precisely in the Mass that this finds its focus. The Mass is the gathering up of man and his whole life and offering it to God in union with the sacrifice of Christ. In the Mass Christ is

really and truly present—just as truly, though in a different
manner, as He once was on the Cross of Calvary. When we
are present at Mass ourselves, provided our dispositions are
what they ought to be, our whole lives are caught up in *His*
life; our day gains a new significance; our actions—even the
most seemingly worthless and indifferent—acquire an eternal
value.'

But there is an interruption. Round the corner of the drive
appears a bicycle, running down the hill much too fast and
wobbling all over the place. As it looms up into the light
thrown by the dining-room windows, it reveals the figure of
Cyril. So fast is he travelling that he misjudges the distance and
crashes head first into the steps. But he doesn't seem hurt; he's
grinning all over his face. And he's holding up a basket,
almost as if it were a victor's trophy. 'Here's your Christmas
dinner. Reared it with me own fair hands, so it ought to be
good.' And peals of laughter. It was an enormous duck.

So Christmas passed, and Lent approached. Week by week
Le Court filled up with the disabled and the helpless; the tempo
of life mounted. To keep the wolf from the door we sold the
flowers, the holly, even the best of the vegetables. To supply
the missing brooms, cutlery and other items of daily household
use, we scoured the surrounding dustbins and dumps—often
with surprising results. To make up for the absence of staff,
we parcelled out the housework among the patients, no one
excluded—not even Granny, who on one occasion was set to
peeling potatoes in bed. To avoid the cost of fitting bells we
grouped those who needed help at night into adjoining rooms
and I slept on the floor outside their door. Even so their hand-
bells and shouts often enough went unheard, and one or other
of those who had come to end their days in peace and quiet
found himself struggling out of bed in the middle of the night
to wake a sleeping watchman. Yet, in spite of it all, in spite
even of the perpetual disorganization that seemed to reign, no
one appeared any the worse. Almost, one would be tempted to

suppose, the better for it, the stronger even in body for having discovered that they were needed and that someone depended on them.

The doctor who attended us argued that we were not equipped for such work, that we should confine ourselves to those who were just a little infirm and needed shelter and food. But necessity, not choice, was our guide. Of those who appealed for help, we asked, first whether they were genuinely in need, second whether they would genuinely be better off in Le Court than anywhere else available. If yes, then we took them, provided only that no harm to the other patients would ensue. At all costs, we decreed, accept the demands that Providence makes, and at all costs complete the day's duties before going to bed. If a duty remains unfulfilled and the hands to do it are literally not available, then press-gang someone into it. Anyone—a patient, a passing visitor, a calling trades-man, but at least someone. If a forgotten duty is remembered in the middle of the night, then up and do it. Anything so long as today's quota is not carried over to tomorrow, for Providence has foreseen each minute from before the begin-ning of the world, and behind all that It disposes there is a design. To each day it has allocated so many duties, so many opportunities, and the necessary means and help to fulfil them. Just enough, no more. It has appointed a season for sowing, and a season for reaping; a time for activity, and a time for rest, a moment of birth and a moment of death. And to each of these it has allotted its particular grace and its particular strength. Ours, then, not to reason how or why; not to say, I have no money, no time, no strength, no health, I will do it later. But to spring to the occasion, to say, I WILL. I will, because I recognize that Providence is calling.

In the coming months these calls for help came from many different directions. From the very doctor who was so opposed to our taking the dying, an elderly lady, yellow like Arthur and every bit as frail, living alone in a local council house, too weak and ill to cook her own food, and with an open, festering cancer which needed twice daily cleaning and dressing. From Liss, a retired housekeeper suffering from heart trouble and perpetually afraid that everything we did for her would make her worse. From our own village of Empshott a bedridden widow partially out of her mind, covered with bedsores and incontinent. Had it not been for Ted French, a forty-year-old Post Office cable layer, in plaster from the waist upwards with his right arm fixed rigidly above his shoulder, who could none the less handle anything from a sack of coke to a bumper for polishing floors, the household routine might well have broken down altogether. But always, by hook or by crook, we managed to scrape through.

Then there was the day when two urgent applications came one after the other. In the morning a letter from a fifteen-stone paralysed man who was about to be sent home to his wife in a fourth-storey flat; in the evening a deputation from the British Legion on behalf of an ex-Marine in the final stages of meningitis. His wife, who was sixty-five years old and crippled, lived in an antiquated village cottage without indoor sanitation or even running water, with no ground-floor room other than the kitchen in which to put her husband. Yet the hospital proposed to send him home at ten the following morning, and nothing that the Legion could do had succeeded in making them change their decision.

When the deputation had left, those who could walk assembled in the huge oak-panelled lounge, lit now by two pressure Tilleys instead of the old wick lamps, and the issue was thrashed out. For once feelings ran high, and though there was sympathy, mixed with indignation against the hospital authorities, there was little inclination to agree. Where, it was asked, would the money come from? Who in the house was qualified to look after a man dying of meningitis? What would happen to the existing patients already receiving the bare minimum of attention and called upon to work to the limit of their capacity? Or suppose the only fit man in the establishment went ill? Where would everyone be then? Yes, true, but what, one might equally ask, about the crippled old lady with no facilities, with no one to whom she could turn in the night? What about those two men, knowing the strain they were going to impose on their wives, unable to lift a finger to help? And what of our principles, of the whole basis on which we worked?

Finally it was Ted who turned the tide. He said:

'I reckon we've always got by in the past, and we'll get by now. We must take them. Something that we're not expecting will turn up.'

And as it so happened something *did* turn up, for neither of the men ever reached Le Court. The first died peacefully in hospital; the second in the ambulance on the way to Liss, each in his own way, having said: 'Now that I know I won't be the death of my wife, I can die in peace.'

On June 28th we set about preparing two special rooms. One was for Frances Jeram, a trained hospital almoner who had offered to come full-time—our first qualified and fully fit helper. The other was for Rosalind Kempson, an advanced case of T.B. who had applied for admission from Singapore. She had travelled as far as Switzerland by sea and rail, and now, after three months' treatment in a sanatorium (though to no good avail), was coming on by air. But the day passed without her making an appearance. Late at night she telephoned to say that the airline company, after having seen her medical report and agreed in writing to take her, had changed their minds at the last moment and sent her back from the airport. The hotel was unwilling to keep her for more than one night, her money was running out, she couldn't get a refund on her ticket. What was she to do?

The seconds were passing; upstairs there were twenty-eight patients waiting to be settled down for the night; the operator was cutting in to say: 'Your time is up'; a trembling voice from the other end was calling out: 'What shall I do? Tell me what to do.'

'Stay where you are and wait. Someone will come and

fetch you.' Then, just as the receiver was going down, a sudden dreadful thought: 'But just a minute. Where are you? WHERE ARE YOU? Ah, at the Excelsior in Zürich.'

But as it turns out Rosalind is not at the Excelsior. In the excitement of the moment she has given the wrong hotel, and it is lunchtime the following day before I can run her to earth. By this time it is clear that the Company cannot be prevailed upon to reverse their decision. They point out that they have a reputation for safe flying, and that—doctor's reports or not—they cannot take risks with people as ill as Mrs. Kempson. Neither can they offer any alternative suggestion. They would like to refund the fare, of course, but regulations preclude cash refunds over the counter. A visit to the railway station proves equally useless. There are no seats to be had at all—not until the end of the week. It is the season; one should foresee these things in advance and book ahead. So one falls upon the last line of defence and calls on the British Consul. But His Excellency is unusually busy and one has to make three visits before obtaining an interview. . . . Even at that the interview leads to nothing.

These reverses, however, have one unexpected effect. They succeed in exciting the sympathy of the hotel keeper who has evidently succumbed to the influence of the frail-looking lady, flushed about the cheekbones and propped up in bed, but with such a determined, hopeful look in her eyes. He can see that she has but one ambition—to end her days in her native land—and so he comes down to the station in person; he is sure that the station master has a heart that one can touch. And such is the case. The station master discovers he has, after all, a berth—just one. He can find no objection to a seriously ill patient travelling by train. He phones ahead to Lyons and Calais telling them to be ready with a wheelchair and attendants.

When we return to the hotel and break the news, there is a triumphant gleam in Rosalind's eyes. We must celebrate, she says. And celebrate we do, in a downstairs alcove prepared for the occasion by the hotel manager. No use saying: 'But we're running out of money. Really I don't need all this. One course and some fruit would have been plenty.' (For the fact is that the only way of getting from London to Zürich was to talk the airline company—at 7.30 a.m.—into accepting a dud cheque, and unless something is done about it tomorrow it will bounce.) No use, when she proudly produces a gift box of 200 cigarettes, protesting: 'But I've given them up; I really don't want to start again.' This is a special occasion, she declares, and there's a hard journey ahead; you need some fortifying.

She is right; it is a hard journey. But when we draw in to Victoria Station, lo and behold, an ambulance is waiting. Now at last one can relax, even lie back, for Rosalind suddenly seems to have been imbued with new strength and life. As we drive along the Hog's Back she sits at the window and starts gesticulating wildly. We stop. She is lifted out and put on a chair looking southwards towards the Downs, and the ambulance men are refreshed with a cup of tea. A pity the airline company cannot see her face now; perhaps if they could they might have thought it worth while not just flying her home, but actually paying for the privilege of doing so. But the loss is theirs. At Greatham corner we unexpectedly pass Mother and Father and manage to flag them. They are in the process of moving house from Greywalls to Le Court Estate, where they propose to settle down and help as best they can. They talk to Mrs. Kempson, welcome her as if to her own home. Seeing them there brings back a flood of boyhood memories; Le Court has suddenly become home in a double sense. At the front door there is a small reception committee headed by Frances, beaming all over her face and obviously well in her element. Rosalind's room is prepared and ready; there are flowers on the dressing-table; the swallows and martins have arrived, they are swooping and zooming outside the window. England, one can see from her expression, has come up to expectations. But this is not all. Downstairs, on the office desk, is a letter from

Lady Cholmondeley with a cheque for £40 'to cover the expenses of the trip'.

So long as we stuck to our established principle, all went well. No doubt we had to keep long hours; no doubt we made do without things that formerly we had looked upon as essential; no doubt we had our moments of anxiety when it looked as if the position was lost; no doubt we improvised in ways which the medical profession would have had difficulty in sanctioning. Yet, in spite of it all nothing went seriously wrong; the means and the help always seemed to be at hand. But as time went on and the work grew, we tended to become over-confident and to take things for granted; we ran up weekly bills, instead of buying only what we could pay for in cash; we became over-hasty in accepting the stories of those who applied for admission, instead of making certain that they really had no alternative; worse still we toyed with plans and schemes purely of our own devising instead of confining ourselves day by day to the work and opportunities in hand. Thus gradually the due order of Providence began to be upset. To the day which It had planned, and for which (in spite of all appearances to the contrary) It would have supplied the strength and the wherewithal, were added unnecessary, and even contradictory duties; time and energy that, properly conserved, would have sufficed for the daily round were dissipated in other directions and only made good by cutting still further into sleep; beds and equipment that should have been available for those really in need were already in use for those who could have found elsewhere to go.

And so gradually the machine began to run down. This was the opportunity for which Father Clarke and others had been looking. Do you, they asked, have any right to take on commitments that, if you go ill or have an accident, will have to pass to others? Don't you know that the Church favours normality and disfavours abnormality? That for a man with your upbringing and background to set himself up as a nurse (and rather a doubtful one at that) is not exactly normal? Haven't you heard that sanctity consists not in doing the extraordinary, but in doing the ordinary extraordinarily well? Can't you see that having got as far as this and having started a work that is obviously good, your duty is to hand it over to someone who knows what he is doing, and yourself to move on to other fields? Don't you think it would be better to settle down and marry? Marriage, after all, is the normal state for those who aren't priests or religious. You are free to do so, for the Church doesn't recognize divorce, and, in Her sight, your own marriage was null and void, for Constance had a husband before you married her; you may never go back to her. So think it over.

A sudden attack of 'flu, necessitating a spell in bed with Mother to fuss over me and keep me quiet, and I did begin to think. Things, after all, were undergoing a change. Frances was there to do the administration, a State Registered Nurse had come to take charge of the nursing, and a committee had been formed to help with the organization. Life, no doubt, was still far from being a sinecure, but it was easing up. One could afford to go to bed for a day or two, at least until the worst of the fever was over; one could afford a certain amount of quiet reading, and just thinking about nothing in particular. One could even afford a holiday with Father Clarke in the rugged wilds of the Island of Skye.

But having once eased up, it was difficult to pick oneself up, difficult to regain the old pace. The first bout of 'flu was followed by another. Then yet another. Advice flowed in profusion. The doctor ordered rest, and so did most of those who called to visit. I went first to my uncle in Paris, and later to the incomparable Abbey of Solesmes. As I did so, values began to change; new horizons came into sight; old ones receded. On the one hand I saw the dignity of all human endeavour and work, in whatever field it might be; on the other the supreme vocation of a life wholly dedicated to prayer. So gradually the pendulum began to swing. It swung first here, then there, at times violently, at others imperceptibly, until, after thirty long months, Providence came to the rescue.

At the outset it had been painful to let go of the reins, even just one of them, and even more painful still to find that others could handle it better than oneself. But far from losing from the new routine, the household seemed to be gaining. Disorder and insecurity were giving way to stability and order; competent helpers were coming forward; the committee was gaining confidence. I found myself thinking that the time had come to change my role, to leave the administration to others, and concentrate on the one essential—maintaining the right spirit. From there it was an easy job to conclude that the proper course of action was to settle down and take a job. And this I did.

But in January 1951, when working on a research project into supersonic flight in the extreme south of Cornwall, there suddenly came an urgent appeal for help. It was from a young epileptic, in his early twenties, an ex-frogman, who was being turned out of one boarding-house after another. Le Court could not take him, partly because they were completely full, but partly because of fear of danger to the other patients. Yet so appealing was his letter that one could hardly let it go just at that. So down on the wilds of the Lizard Peninsula, in the abandoned and derelict Station Headquarters of what had once been R.A.F. Predannack, there sprung up a second Home, St. Teresa's, this time with a committee of its own from the very beginning. For a while things ran well, and with the working week devoted to the job and my spare time divided between St. Teresa's and Le Court, the days passed quickly and happily. But the New Year brought certain developments. To St. Teresa's came a former bomber pilot, now suffering from schizophrenia, who was neither ill enough to be put in a mental home, nor well enough to look after himself and whose mother was breaking down under the strain of caring for him single-handed. But it was soon found that he did not fit in with the others and that he would either have to be sent back or else a separate home found for him. To send him back was impossible, and so we commandeered the old W.A.A.F. Officers' Mess and set to work to convert it into our third Home—Holy Cross, as it was re-named.

There was little peace. At Le Court the crack in the walls that had once so worried Pat Weddell was beginning to widen, and the house was rapidly becoming unsafe for habitation. On a conservative estimate £9,000 would be required to stop any further subsidence, and heaven only knows how much to build a new house elsewhere in the grounds. The family was growing, and its needs multiplying beyond the point of merely part-time attention. So I gave up the job.

And meanwhile life was becoming a struggle. It was a struggle to get up, a struggle to work, a struggle to decide the future, a struggle to know how to accept all those who were calling out for help. For the problem was, how to be in more than one place at once? And even if one could find a way, even if one could manage to be in two places at once, or, better still, ten thousand; even if one could succeed in housing all the sick all over the world and giving them all shelter; even if all this and yet more besides, was it enough? Was there not some hidden depth in suffering, some unseen yearning in the sufferer, that called for more than merely shelter and physical relief?

So no wonder, perhaps, that one should waver in one's tracks; that one should desire better to understand the mystery and power of suffering in order the better to be able to help those who suffer; and that one should turn to the cloister, to those who retire from the turmoil of the world in order to pray for its peace, as the one means of doing so. For has it not been said that we should work as if everything depended on us, and pray as if everything depended on God? Then would not the ideal arrangement be for the committees and staff to run the Homes, and for myself to enter the cloister and learn to pray?

Then, on August 20th, 1952, the fourth anniversary of

Arthur's death, Providence stepped in. A visiting priest found me in bed for the morning and, brushing aside the doctor's verdict that it was just another attack of 'flu, carted me bodily off to St. Michael's Hospital, Hayle, to be X-rayed. There, while drinking a cup of coffee in the waiting-room and awaiting the result of the picture, the door burst open and in rushed an extraordinary apparition dressed from toe to neck in white, with a green towel wrapped round his head. Presumably the doctor. In the broken English of a Pole labouring under emotion he said: 'Captain Cheshire, it's very serious, very serious indeed. . . . No, please don't laugh. It's nothing to laugh about at all.' Perhaps not—whatever IT might be. But HE was—with that extraordinary headgear, and looking so deadly serious. 'What have you still got to do?' (My God, what a question!) 'I mean what have you got to clear up now, this minute, that you can't leave to someone else?'

'As it so happens, nothing.'

'But there must be something; letters, at least.'

'No, as it so happens a voluntary typist turned up out of the blue last night just as I was thinking of going to bed; and she insisted on keeping going for most of the night. Said it was the last chance she would have. And so we cleared the In-tray—right to the bottom.'

'Then you'll go straight to bed.' A little embarrassed pause. He suddenly became aware of the towel and took it off. 'Captain Cheshire, you've got T.B. of the lungs. We'll get a bed ready for you, and once you're in it there you'll have to stay.'

And stay I did—for the best part of two and a half years.

In the New Year, after I had been moved to Midhurst Sanatorium, Sussex, they took me across to the surgical block for a series of operations on my lung—a new experience to have to lie back and let others do the doing. On the eve of the first of them a life-sized reproduction of the Holy Face from the Shroud of Turin was put on the wall at the foot of my bed. And there, for a full month, I did little but lie and look at it. Here, too, was a new experience. For in front of me was no face such as artists depict, even the best of them, but one that stood in a class all of its own, one that bore the unmistakable stamp of authenticity—the face of the dead Christ, not painted by an artist's hand, but imprinted by some mysterious process of natural photography on the winding-sheet in which He had been buried. Here was not just a face worthy of a God who had become man out of love for man, who had lived as only God can live, who had taught as only Truth itself can teach, who had died and then risen from the dead as only the author of life could rise; here was a face which had plumbed to the very depths the mystery of suffering and death. As I gazed at it I felt impelled to enquire into its origin, and as I enquired I felt impelled not so much to go on looking (though that I certainly did), as to get up and act.

For here before my eyes was the Face of Victory; the Face of One who acknowledges no defeat; who, though overwhelmed by pain, yet stands firm and unmoved; who, though done to death, has yet conquered even this last enemy; who has seen in suffering and death, not mere misfortunes to be put up with as best they might, but as the very instruments of the world's salvation, even as the heaven-sent means of redeeming a fallen humanity. Here was a face which summoned each and everybody, whether in the cloister or in the factory, whether in the forest or in the office, whether in the house or on a sick bed, to take his share in the battle, to be fellow conquerors with Him in the conquest of Heaven. Here was a face which spoke on behalf of all those who had already laid down their lives, of whatever nationality, better men than we who have survived, whose sufferings and courage cry out to us to carry on where they left off, not nation against nation, but the entire human race against our common enemy, against the forces of error and darkness, against divisions and prejudice, against all that bars the way to that eternal and boundless happiness for which man is destined. And here was a face which guaranteed victory in advance, which demanded only that we should stand firm where we were put and leave the rest to Him.

Before such a face as this, so ill used, yet so serene, so majestic yet so gentle, who could fail to be moved? Who could fail to see its reflection in the poor, the maimed, the sick, the dying, the unwanted, the lonely, in all those who suffer or are in need from whatever cause? And who, having seen all this, could be content to lie back and rest so long as anywhere in the world there remains but one human being in want or distress?

EPILOGUE

IN spring 1954, whilst still in Midhurst, I was invited to go to India and see what could be done for the incurably sick out there. It was not perhaps the most propitious moment of moments, for there was a fourth operation still to come and no guarantee even when it was over that all would be well. Nonetheless the invitation was far too sincere and appealing to believe that it had been received merely in order to be refused, and so, for better or for worse, I accepted it. After all, no one is indispensable, and even supposing that I were unable to go myself someone would surely be found to step into the breach. Then nine months later, armed with many instructions and warnings, I was given my discharge.

To begin with the going was slow, but the course of 1955 saw a steady acceleration, and by early November, when the first four of us landed in Bombay, a good deal had happened on the English front. New Homes had been started at Bromley in Kent, at East Preston in Sussex, at Ampthill in Bedfordshire and at Staunton Harold in Leicestershire, in each case with virtually nothing in the bank and depending upon the good-will of a handful of men and women who had come forward and offered to take over the full responsibility. At Le Court the old building had been replaced by a new one costing £67,000 and given by the Carnegie Trust. At St. Teresa's, thanks to the widespread support from the whole of Cornwall, new premises were going up in ideal surroundings on the shores of Penzance Bay. In London, as a result of Father's persistent efforts, a charitable Trust had been formed and registered, which was now the body legally responsible for supervising and co-ordinating the work of the local committees. Behind the scenes, anxious that personal attention and affection should not be swamped by organization, Mother had become the friend and companion of the patients.

But good though all this was, there were still calls for help that the Trust was unable to answer simply because they did not come within the scope of the Homes. There were people with personal problems looking for help within the framework of their own daily lives; there were the jailbirds who, for one reason or another, could not settle into normal surroundings; there were those who were just lost and aimless, and who were looking for someone to give them shelter and direction. None of these activities were covered by the aims and objects of the Trust Deed, few were within our personal competence, and the majority were so much a matter of personal care and attention—not to mention dedication and calling—that it was difficult to see how they could be supervised by committees or trusts.

Then, on rather a cold and dreary Ampthill afternoon, there appeared Sue Ryder, a slightly built, tired-looking girl hardly thirty years old, recently known to television audiences throughout the country for her work on behalf of the Stateless and disabled survivors of Nazi atrocities. During the war she had been a member of the Special Forces in Europe, and since then had devoted her life to these forgotten allies whom the tide of German aggression had left stranded and unwanted in the very country that had caused their terrible sufferings. To her, who had lived in their camps for the past ten years and had watched the methods of the official relief organizations, with their vast resources and their sheaf upon sheaf of case numbers, it was personal service and personal respect for the indivudual that must take precedence over everything else, whatever the cost. And of how great the cost had been there were ample signs on her face.

As time went on we met, now in one of the Homes, now down at Cavendish in Suffolk where her own sixteenth-century house had been turned into a place of refuge for some of the hardest hit of the survivors, and exchanged ideas and plans for extending our respective works into new areas, particularly into Eastern Europe where it was reported that there was overwhelming need. But opportunities for meeting were few and far between, for apart from anything else India was fast looming up, and there was much to be done and arranged.

Shortly before we left for Bombay, the long-forgotten *Bomber Pilot* yielded an unexpected dividend with the result that we succeeded not only in paying for our passages but also in buying a Land Rover and some essential equipment. But in actual cash we set foot on Indian soil with less than £100 in our pockets, and this we lost in Customs with everything we had brought. Then, by the grace of God, a small plot of jungle was offered to us on a pay-when-you-can basis, and on January 2nd, 1956, leaving Margot Mason in Bombay to battle with officialdom, we moved into a three-roomed asbestos hut given and erected by a local builder, and which, because it had been born at Christmas, we called Bethlehem House.

At first we bemoaned the loss of the Land Rover and redoubled our efforts to extricate it from its Customs prison, but soon we discovered that we were almost better off without it, for those who have very little and are forced to fetch and carry on their own backs and dig trenches with their own hands are more readily taken to be poor, and thus more easily obtain help. And such was our experience. Yet even so there were difficulties looming up on the horizon. The Home, situated as it was on top of a small hill and commanding a fine view of the surrounding countryside (and slums), was a haven of peace and beauty to those who lived and worked in it, both patients and staff. But the newly formed committee, which held its first meeting on a packing-case under a mango tree, was less interested in views and aesthetics than it was in such practical considerations as water, access and finance. Water, they maintained, was never to be found on top of hills in India; the earth track that was being used at present in lieu of a road would be washed away within the first week of the monsoon; there were seven patients already installed in the Home, with the prospect of unlimited numbers of others to follow, no trained nurse to look after them, and nowhere to house her if one should suddenly appear; and there was virtually no money at all in the bank. What, they politely enquired, was to be done? Sitting amongst the committee was Nina Carney, our one and only contact when we had landed in Bombay. Perhaps she considered herself more personally implicated, since it was largely thanks to her that the land had been found and the asbestos hut acquired; or perhaps she felt a special bond of sympathy with Pop, as he had been nicknamed, the old Southern Indian from Malabar who had been picked off the streets in an advanced stage of cancer, and who now, for the first time in thirty-five years, had found a home that he could truly call his own. But at any rate she jumped to her feet and answered: 'I know. My husband will put on a pantomime.'

Jimmy Carney, as he was fond of repeating, was a practical Yorkshire engineer, who did not hold with starting hospitals without a farthing in the bank and in places where there was neither access nor hope of water. Nevertheless he rose to the occasion with a will. When the monsoon broke, he obtained the use of a 10,000-gallon water tank, manhandled it up through the mile of jungle, and connected it to improvised gutters on the roof, with the result that the Home had sufficient water for its essential needs until well into the New Year. Then he got down to the problems of access and by devious ways succeeded in carving an emergency track along higher ground which at least brought the more intrepid drivers to within wading distance of the gates. Finally he set to work on the pantomime. He pieced together a home-made script, borrowed one of the most beautiful gardens in Bombay, built his own stage, collected the cast from where he could, and commissioned Nina to make the costumes. From start to finish it was all home-made and all voluntary, and if on the opening night, with the Governor in attendance, some of us were found to be in a certain state of trepidation, no doubt we had an excuse. But we need not have worried. So well was the pantomime received that it had to be put on for a further four nights after Christmas, and was classed by the Press as one of the social hits of Bombay. In solid cash it won £3,000, but more important still was the goodwill it attracted. Amongst the distinguished visitors who came to see it was a Minister of State who had seen a pantomime as a small boy in London, and had always looked forward to the day when he could see another. Now that his wish had been granted, he called us together and asked what we needed most for the Home. We answered, a road. And eighteen months later we received it.

But long before then, growing tired of interminable and fruitless schemes for solving the water problem, and faced with the needs of twenty-two patients, three fully trained Spanish nurses and two or three Indian staff, Jimmy, the practical Yorkshire engineer, threw yet another contractor's report into the waste-paper basket and decided to make his own bore on the site itself. He picked on a one-man firm whose sole piece of equipment was an antiquated two-stroke engine and dragooned him into setting to work. At six feet the drill hit rock, and the man gave it up. But Jimmy was not having any of that.

'All I want you to do,' he said, 'is to bore. Just bore. When I want you to stop, I'll tell you.' And so the contractor returned to his work, not just for a week, nor just for a month, but from early February 1957 until well into April. At intervals he found the monotony—and no doubt, as he concluded, the futility—too much for him; but Jimmy's determination was no less adamant than the hidden rocks against which the drill was battling, and it was all to no avail. Then one morning, at a depth where no two-stroke boring machine of that vintage can ever have penetrated before, he struck water—perhaps not water in unlimited quantities, but at least sufficient to hold disaster at bay until help should arrive. And today, as these closing lines are being written, there has unexpectedly appeared at the bottom of the road a load of piping, delivered by a friendly Municipality in preparation for the mains supply which is to follow. Help has come; the battle has been won, and now that Sue Ryder's work for the Forgotten Allies has broken through into Eastern Europe where few, if any, British have been privileged to work since the last war, and where an immense fund of goodwill and generosity lies waiting to be mobilized for the peace and unity of mankind, the gateway has been opened—so it seems—to almost every country in the world.

Our own small victories—even though in fact it be others who have played the principal part in winning them—always loom large in our thoughts and memory; and no doubt we attach more importance to them than we should. But these are not personal victories. They are the victories of the self-sacrifice and fundamental goodness of many men and women of every denomination, religion, and class, most of them without overmuch of this world's goods, but all of whom have been touched like Jimmy and Nina by the needs of the sick and the homeless, and who, whilst still remaining true to their own beliefs and ideals, have acknowledged by their actions our universal membership of the one human family. And indeed peace and unity are not the concern only of Prime Ministers and Governments; they are not won by force of arms, nor even by a masterly stroke of statesmanship; rather are they built up brick by brick by all of us, each according to our means and our opportunities, in the measure in which we bring peace and unity into our immediate surroundings.

But above all these are the victories of all those who suffer and are in need, and who thus share so pre-eminently in the redemptive victory of the Cross. The closer we stay to them, the greater will be the good we achieve, the more easily will fall the barriers that so divide us, the more fully will we understand how 'No man is an island entire of itself. Every man is a part of the continent, a part of the main. Any man's death diminishes me, because I am involved in mankind.'

APPENDIX A

THE RYDER CHESHIRE MISSION FOR THE RELIEF OF SUFFERING

Non-denominational and depending upon voluntary help and contributions, the Mission forms a family, or 'Commonwealth', of the following entirely separate and autonomous Foundations, more of which, it is hoped, will follow. A special point is made of keeping administrative costs down to the minimum.

I SUE RYDER FORGOTTEN ALLIES

Hon. Treasurers:
    G. D. Levack, Esq., F.C.A.
    H. Ince, Esq.

Hon. Secretaries:
    Miss P. Bains
    Miss D. Urbaniec

Following the relief work started in 1945 in many camps, hospitals, and prisons for the Stateless victims of Nazism, there is today still much individual case-work throughout Germany, in addition to the following:

Home for Concentration Camp Survivors. Cavendish, Suffolk
140 Forgotten Allies are brought each year from the Continent for a complete holiday and to join those already resettled there.

St. Christopher Settlement. Grossburgwedel, Hanover
Secretary: Mr. Jerzy Budkiewicz.
Eight homes and several flats, built mostly by international teams of volunteers for those whose health is broken.

St. Christopher Kreis. Berlinerstrasse, Frankfurt a.m.

Chairman: H. H. Princess Margaret of Hesse und bei Rhein.

Since 1945 Sue Ryder has been personally responsible for the visiting, after-care, and rehabilitation of the Stateless boys in German prisons, many of them convicted for reprisals against their former torturers.

Homes for the Sick in Poland

Chairman of the Committee: Direktor Snieguki, Ministry of Health, Warsaw.

Prefabricated buildings, each containing forty beds and costing £5,000, are sent from England to relieve the distress of the Forgotten Allies.

Four established at Konstancin, Zyrardow, Naleczow, and Garwolin. Two in process of erection at Helenow and Warsaw.

II RAPHAEL, THE RISPANA, DEHRA DUN

Lying in the foothills of the Northern Himalayas, Raphael is the Far Eastern Headquarters of the Mission. From small beginnings in tents in April 1959, it today houses 50 leprosy patients and 30 mentally retarded and homeless children, and is being planned as a whole 'village' of Homes where 600 or more of the incurably sick may lead as full and happy lives as possible.

Hon. Medical Director: Lt.-Gen. K. S. Master, M.C., I.M.S. (Rtd.)
Hon. Secretary: Mrs. A. Dhar.
Hon. Welfare Officer: Mrs. D. Rawlley.

III THE CHESHIRE FOUNDATION HOMES FOR THE SICK

Caring for the incurable and homeless sick (mostly in the younger age-group), they are autonomously run by local committees within the general aims and principles of the Foundation. In each country there is a central trust which owns all the properties, presides over the Homes, and is the source of the committees' authority. Average number of patients when Home complete: thirty.

Kenmore, Scott Lane, Cleckheaton, Yorkshire.

*West Midland Home, Penn, Wolverhampton, Staffordshire.

*The London Cheshire Home at Dulwich, College Road, London, S.E.21.

Holme Lodge, West Bridgford, Nottingham.

*The Hill, Sandbach, Cheshire.

*Holehird House, Windermere, Westmorland.

*Marske Hall, near Redcar, Yorkshire.

*The Mote House, Maidstone, Kent.

*Greenhill House, Timsbury, near Bath, Somerset.

Holy Cross, Mullion, Cornwall, was handed over in 1953 to Major (Mrs.) Shelagh Howe, who has managed it ever since entirely on her own initiative.

Eire

An Irish Trust is in the process of being formed.

Ardeen, Shillelagh, Co. Wicklow.

India

Trustees: Rajkumari Amrit Kaur, T. N. Jagadisan, J. A. K. Martyn, O.B.E. (Chairman elect), Sir Dhiren Mitra, Col. L. Sawhny (Chairman retiring), Brigadier Virendra Singh.

Hon. Treasurer: Y. S. Tayal.

Enquiries to: P.O. Box 518, Calcutta.

Bethlehem House, Andheri, Bombay.

Shanti Rani House, 13 Upper Strand Road, Serampore, West Bengal.

Govind Bhawan, 16 Pritam Road, Dehra Dun, U.P.

Vrishanti Illam, Katpadi Township, N. Arcot (founded by Mrs. P. Chinnadorai for burnt-out leprosy patients).

Rustomji P. Patel Cheshire Home, Sundernagar, Jamshedpur, Bihar (crippled children).

Banarsidas Chandiwala Swasthya Sadan, Kalkaji, New Delhi.

Anbu Nilayan, Covelong, Madras.

†The Cheshire Home, Poona.

†The Cheshire Home, Bangalore.

* In process of preparation.
† In process of construction.

APPENDIX B

The Holy Shroud is a 15 ft. long linen sheet which has been handed down from generation to generation as the Winding Sheet in which our Lord Jesus Christ was buried, and is now preserved in Turin. On it can be seen the life-size imprint of a man, both front and back, who has not only died by crucifixion but has suffered all that history records of Christ—and only of Christ. This imprint is in negative form, and is only decipherable when reversed on a photographic plate. In sixty years of research science has not found one valid objection to make, and although the subject remains shrouded in mystery it may be said with certainty that the imprint is not the work of human hands. Amongst the many publications which refer, the following are two of the better-known for English readers:

Self Portrait of Christ. E. A. WUENSCHEL, C.SS.R. New York, 1954. Price 7s. 6d.

The Shroud of Turin. English translation of *Das Grabtuch von Turin*, WERNER BULST, S.J., Frankfurt, 1955. Bruce Publishing Company, Milwaukee, U.S.A. Price 36s.

Further information from 7 Market Mews, London, W.1.